I0187929

JAILHOUSE CONFIDENTIAL:
on the inside looking in

*An unusual look inside Rikers Island from an
officer's perspective in the 1970's.
Some names have been changed to protect the guilty.*

PETER KOUTSOUKOS

RED
PENGUIN
Books

Jailhouse Confidential

Copyright © 2020 by Peter Koutsoukos

All rights reserved

Published by Red Penguin Books

Bellerose Village, New York

Library of Congress Control Number: 2020924301

ISBN

Print 978-1-952859-89-2 / 978-1-63777-012-2

Digital 978-1-952859-90-8

No part of this book may be reproduced in any form or by any electronic or mechanical means, including information storage and retrieval systems, without written permission from the author, except for the use of brief quotations in a book review.

To the 'Boldest'

To all the men and women who chose to do a job that many have feared to do. Over the decades there were many changes and procedures that have enhanced the prisoners lives behind bars while they await trial. I wonder if there were any significant changes that would have enhanced the officer's safety behind the gates. I know what hasn't changed, when you cannot spend Christmas or Thanksgiving with your loved ones when duty calls.

When in contact with prisoners, danger always lurks. Many times, you are forced to work a double shift to ensure there are enough officers to respond to potential dangers when the alarm rings.

Remember this. What you do, no one else consciously thinks or cares about. The job you have chosen inherently spells stress that takes a toll on the body and the mind. You will never receive a thank you; but know that you are the silent protector of society. Be proud of your contribution and sacrifices. You deserve to be recognized, but probably never will. Stay well, live long and be strong. To be sure, you are a special breed.

CONTENTS

INTRODUCTION

I survived the twenty-year storm on the 'job' and completed my tour. It's been twenty-five years since my last day on the tiers. Perhaps enough time has passed to share my experiences from the 'rock', objectively. Some who have told their stories, did not. They only tasted the bitterness and were unable to endure the total journey through the good, bad and strange events in this world of iron and concrete.

Reactions to these accounts by tenured university professors, a retired firefighter, members of law enforcement and others, range from fascination and bewilderment, to disbelief.

I still face the memories, and twisted emotions from my jailhouse experiences. The lessons learned and bonds made continue to shape my life. They are constant reminders of where I have been, and how I made it here.

PREFACE

By the time I met Peter Koutsoukos, he had already completed serving his sentence—20 years to life. Pete was a correction officer in New York City's Department of Correction. He started his career on Rikers Island, a 413-acre secure complex that sits in the East River between Queens and the Bronx. The facilities on this island house an inmate population of 10,000. Pete dedicated 20 years of his life to the custody, control, and care of the city's most violent criminal offenders. Two years after he began his employment, Rikers had the distinction of being one of the top three most dangerous institutions in the nation.

In the United States, there are an estimated 2,000,000 sworn law enforcement officers, less than 150,000 are correction officers.

These men and women spend 100% of their duty time in direct contact with violent offenders, individuals committing crimes such as assault, robbery, rape, and murder. These officers never fire their weapons because they are prohibited from carrying firearms in their workplace.

So, the question presents itself: Where does this special breed of human being come from, these men and women who choose to incarcerate themselves alongside prisoners, perpetrators of crimes against society, harmful, illegal, and immoral acts? Unlike the majority of law enforcers that live and work in the midst of the general population, correction officers must prevail within the criminal element of society.

Here, within the pages of Pete's memoirs, we get a hint at the answer to our question. It seems that these rare caretakers are created right in our midst, hidden from our eyes in the common lives of ordinary people. Children growing up with us and before us in plain sight.

Pete's time as a prison guard became the dark side of his life. After all, he was one of those people, the ones we didn't quite get.

That tribe of brave men and women who voluntarily give years of their lives to protect criminals from themselves and each other, while always keeping them apart from us.

The lessons learned and bonds made created the man we see in these pages. The memories and the twisted emotions from prison still impact his life.

Rick Monsour

ON THE JOB

I work in Corrections, the money is good.
It's one of those jobs the public really never understood.
It comes with its tension and ups and downs.
Working with professionals and sometimes with clowns.
My job can turn dangerous at the drop of a hat.
You'd best be aware and know where your partner is at.
The tier is where the job is, that's where you learn your sixth sense.
Appearing cool and collected is all there is for my defense.
They say in twenty years I could leave and get a pension.
But for now I must find ways to relieve all this tension.
Maybe I'll leave before this twenty is through.
Find something better that's different and new.
For now this is it, I have all this to think about.
Trying to be careful, and not be taken out.
I'll give it my best, to do what I do.
But just remember I'm a correction officer, not a hack or a screw.

There are times in life when significant changes occur. These set you in a new direction. My life started to change at 22 years old. I was entering a whole new world.

CLIMATE CHANGE

B ack in the 1970s, and even earlier, times were different. In school, if you needed to be disciplined for cursing, teachers would put soap in your mouth, as my mother did to me. In Catholic school, the nuns would hit your palms with a stick. My teacher, Mr. Seidel, would whip your hiney with a rubber-tipped pointer. Nicking your ass by swinging it closer and closer, until he just pinched the tip of your skin with your pants still on, of course. The girls never got the stick. None of this could happen today.

It was the same deal working the jails in that era. Too many inmates were being treated at hospitals for allegedly assaulting officers. If you think about it, it seems it should've been the other way around. That's when the Board of Corrections was established, to oversee what the hell was going on inside these institutions. It was a different time, and it explains a lot about how these events took place.

ON THE JOB TRAINING / A SCAR
FOR LIFE

I am a retired captain of the NYCD. In 1972 at the age of 22, I became a NYC Correction Officer. I began my career on Rikers Island at the old House of Detention for Men. James A. Thomas, for whom the facility was named, was our warden. He was a tall, confident black man who always had a large cigar hanging out of the side of his mouth. Many of my fellow officers, including myself, have many memories of this particular facility. It was the oldest jail on the "Rock," and it was straight out of an old Cagney movie. The old iron tiers, three rows high, twelve in each block. Painted and repainted a million times. I believe much of our character and our way of thinking has to do with that experience. We were a tight-knit group. Black, White, Hispanic and Asian officers. There wasn't any tension or animosity between us. We joked openly to each other about race, and no one was ever offended. Whether we were eating in the mess hall, walking down the corridor, or coming and going from the locker room, we all became one in response to an alarm; and there were many each day.

During the 1975 riot, we spent 18 hours together when the inmates held six officers hostage. It was tense, and every imaginable emotion went through us all. Fear, anger, bravado, and frustration; we felt it all. It was mentally exhausting. I missed becoming a hostage by one hour. I was to be the 7B officer's relief that night at 11:00 p.m. He was taken hostage at 10:00 p.m. The inmates soaped down the floors, ripped out toilets and sinks to toss down on us from the tiers. They barricaded the entrances, giving themselves more time to prepare for war. In the end, all of the hostages were released unscathed, except for one. Jorge, the Latino officer, wasn't so lucky. His unfair treatment and hatred towards the inmates became a reason for them to mentally and physically abuse him while being held hostage. Jorge divorced soon after, and rumor had it that he became a monk sometime later. This was kept very quiet, but you can imagine the torture and humiliation he was put through.

After millions of dollars in damages, the inmates got what they wanted. Those involved as the ringleaders received amnesty through negotiations.

To this day, if by chance I meet an old friend from that jail, we immediately hug each other because of that special brotherhood. We took a lot, gave a lot, and witnessed some episodes that we would rather forget.

HDM was the place you were sent if you "effed up" in another less-offensive jail. Most of us just picked the short straw and began our careers there. You know that the job changed you as a person when your own mother tells you so.

I still socialize and speak with a handful of these brothers, and we share a special bond. Some became wardens, deputy wardens, tour commanders, and captains, like me. We didn't forget; moreover, we can't forget, those years. They had a profound impact on our lives.

SWORN IN / FIRST LOCKOUT

I t was August of 1972 when it became official. I was now a New York City Correction Officer—a screw, hack, a jail guard. I had just turned 22 and now had a gun and a badge, sporting the shortest haircut since smoking my first joint at the age of 16. This was a whole new life for me. Now I was "The Man," part of the establishment that my generation didn't quite trust. This was a turning point in my life. I felt noticeably different sitting around the coffee table with my friends listening to Pink Floyd and the Vanilla Fudge while passing a water pipe that was filled with good pot and cheap wine. I felt so out of place. Amazing how short hair and being a peace officer could change everything. Pot could make you paranoid, but this was something different. I felt alienated in some way. I didn't look or feel like I fit in. This was my career now, a new chapter in my life. My income had doubled. I did it for job security. During the next 20 years of my life, I had no idea what the real cost would be.

My first assignment was the Adolescent Remand Shelter on Rikers Island. This was for inmates under the age of 18 awaiting trial for their alleged crimes. Built in 1933, it was the oldest housing area on Rikers. The housing areas were called Blocks and numbered from 2-8, including two special housings, 1A and 1B, for protective custody individuals who may not have survived the general population for various reasons. Blocks 2-8 held 250 bodies each, with two inmates living in an 8x6 foot cell and sharing a small sink, metal bunk beds, and one toilet. Imagine living in such tight quarters with someone you were forced to live with.

Another job post was called the rail man, who stood in the long corridor between two blocks that were opposite of each other. No one could enter or exit a block without the rail man's key. This was a security feature to monitor the people in and out. That morning the rail man was Officer Mike Grogan. I had to verify the inmate count before the officer that I was relieving could go home. Now the inmates were to be locked out for recreation, which consisted of TV, checkers, dominos, and pushups in the dayroom.

I was locked behind the gate where the cells were, and it was time to let everyone out of their little iron nests for recreation. Here I was, my first time turning the heavy wheel that would open the cell doors. As I started to release the cell doors and call out "On the Lockout," many inmates poked their heads out requesting to remain locked in their cells. I thought to myself, so far so good.

What happened next was when the reality of it all came to me. I suddenly felt this strange feeling that I'd never had before. Being a rookie and inexperienced, I found out rather quickly why so many wanted to remain safely inside the 8x6. The inmates who had chosen to come out were all curiously carrying something in their hands and were walking towards me approaching the front of the block armed with everything from metal buckets to sharpened homemade shivs and pieces of broken chair parts. They were climbing the eight-foot fence attempting to get to the other side to attack the inmates that were housed on the A side. At the time, I didn't know who they were trying to harm or kill. Was it one of us they wanted? I had to think quickly, and I remembered from training that somewhere in the officer's station there was an alarm button specifically for situations like this, but where was it? I had never been shown. Things were getting scary at this point as some were successfully scaling the fence. Suddenly, I found myself alone. Where were the other officers? Then I remembered that the backup alarm system was to take the station phone off the hook and in seconds the alarm would sound to the control room. I slammed the phone to the ground cracking it. Finally, Grogan, the rail man, saw the situation and said that he'd better let me out. He opened the gate quickly, and I slipped out as he re-secured the gate. Just at that moment, a flood of officers came streaming in with riot sticks, establishing control and ordering everyone who made it over the gate to get on their stomachs and place their hands behind their heads. Now we had control back and ordered all inmates to lock back into their cells.

The next course of action was to search the entire area for contraband and hidden weapons. This included the inmates, the contents of their cells, and all of the outlying areas. We found a few shivs and some hooch, which was the inmate's version of homemade wine. This was usually found in a large plastic garbage bag filled with wet bread, chunks of fruit, and for some reason, old socks. You could smell it a mile away.

Everyone stayed locked in for most of the day, only locking out for meals one tier at a time in order to maintain control. Inmate transfers were carried out to break up the troublemakers and gangs. Some received medical attention. The day ended without any other problems. What else would be coming? That remained to be seen.

That was my first day on the job. This was only the beginning of the sixth sense that I would develop into an art form and that would stick with me for the rest of my life. Only 19 years and 10 months to go.

Sometimes, associating with the wrong people can get you into trouble. Either I was lucky or smart enough to realize my limits by being a follower instead of a leader. Hanging with friends who went a little too far is when my guardian angel would step in to prevent me from the inevitable destruction that lay ahead.

TAKING CHANCES

I think back on the things I participated in with others, and at times, alone. I did more than sleep in the locker room and drive the warden's car off Rikers Island to picnic in Astoria Park, dining on Italian heroes and cannoli. I took advantage of any chance to separate myself from the depressing atmosphere back in the jail. Along with my friend and coworker Eddie, I conjured up an idea to dispose of the accumulated weapons and other contraband off the island. We took the stash to the local sanitation depot, but they refused to accept it. We wound up just dumping our collection right into the East River to join the four-legged rats after confiscating them from the two-legged ones. This turned out to be a good gig. As a result, we scheduled the contraband dump and deli visits as soon as we had enough shivs and other no-no's we accumulated from various searches.

Other officers were doing their thing while on duty, as well. This was the 1970s, and almost everyone would find comfort in getting high on something, whether it was marijuana or alcohol. After work, the black officers would meet on the Queens side of the Rikers bridge and pop their car trunks which seemed like portable bars. They contained whiskey, wine, and ice. The white guys were smoking joints on the way home or meeting at the local gin mill where the beer was cheap.

I've witnessed a straight-laced officer morph into a full-blown heroin addict right before my eyes. The inmates found his weak spot. First, it started with him just bringing in a sandwich for them, then marijuana or stronger dope from a relative or friend. This is called a mule, being the carrier of the drug. Finally, he was shooting up in the cell with the inmate and becoming addicted. It's very sad and disheartening to see a fellow officer in uniform marching past his co-workers at roll call in handcuffs, escorted by two detectives and a deputy warden.

Of course, as we tried absorbing what just happened, the warden stepped up to the podium and read us the riot act. He drove home the message of what could happen if we did not act professionally or were taken advantage of by the ever-scheming individuals we were babysitting.

Then there was a fellow officer Billy. We hung out on occasion, bar hopping. One day on the 5:00 a.m. to 1:00 p.m. shift, Billy was approached by a young black officer called CJ. He asked Billy if he would like to share half of a drug called THC. It stands for Tetrahydrocannabinol, which is the main ingredient found in marijuana. They both smoked marijuana as a recreational drug socially and thought this high could be handled easily for the few hours they had left giving meal relief in the jail. CJ was about one hundred pounds soaking wet and no taller than five foot eight. He sported a large afro hairdo. CJ could have easily passed for a 14-year-old if he shaved the fuzz he was trying to establish on his light-skinned chin.

The drug looked like a tiny oil stain sitting on one sheet of rolling paper. CJ carefully tore the dot in half as best as he could and gave Billy his share. An hour and a half passed since they consumed the alleged THC. It was now 9:30, less than four hours remaining on the shift. Billy's body began to feel very strange, but he was still under control. He had experienced this feeling a few times before. It was before he decided to become a trustworthy, professional correction officer. Billy quickly realized he was on a psychedelic hallucinatory acid high. Worse of all, he was in the middle of a jail surrounded by 150 inmates. He felt like he just dropped into a snake pit with slithering humans milling all around him.

Knowing what this drug can do, he decided to concentrate and get his head together as best he could without freaking out. Billy didn't want to wind up in a hospital sitting in a rubber room. One minute felt like an hour, an hour like a day, taking deep breaths when he remembered.

Suddenly, an inmate approached with a question or request. The inmate took one look into Billy's eyes; they spelled danger. He immediately turned away, thinking he had just peered into eyes that looked strikingly like the demonic gaze of the infamous, "acid head" murderer and cult leader, Charles Manson. That was Billy's perception.

Fighting his body and mind all the way, it was finally the end of the shift and time to go home. Billy got into his four-speed Firebird. He was only five miles from home. Constantly staring at the speedometer as he drove. Making sure the police didn't pull him over or get into an accident.

Prayers were answered. Billy finally made it to the sanctuary of his apartment. He immediately lit up a joint to slow down his high. Hoping it was all a bad dream, he finally fell asleep. As for CJ, he went home sick that day. Deeply shaken by the experience, he was unable to handle the stress, a victim of poor judgment, and the effects of this misrepresented drug. Billy never spoke to CJ again. From then on, he stuck with joints outside the joint.

Now, you might ask how I came to know the details of this event. Well, Billy didn't drive a Firebird, it was a Camaro. Moreover, Billy wasn't Billy.

Billy was me.

Most people go to work every day, running their usual routines. The morning coffee, the same train, expecting all the uneventful chores of the day. Correction officers are not like most people. The only exception is the bad coffee and liver with a curious green tint.

MEN'S HOUSE OF DETENTION

After the adolescent inmates transferred out, we became the Men's House of Detention. The atmosphere changed dramatically when the adults moved in. It was much more relaxed and quieter now. Captain "Hollywood" ordered me to report to Block 3 to guard an inmate. When I arrived, it became obvious Hollywood forgot to tell me that the inmate was dead.

Sprawled in the center of the main level, which we called the "flats," was a body in a pool of blood covered with state-issued gray blankets. Only an arm and a leg were exposed. The face was covered by a blanket. It appeared to be a suicide. The word was that he jumped off the top tier yelling the words "Ma, I'm coming home," then he jumped. Or did he?

All inmates remained locked in and were asked to provide information regarding what they heard or saw. No one said much to confirm if it was suicide or if he was thrown off the tier. Now, I had to stay there and wait for the Medical Examiner to arrive to officially declare the death. While I waited and stood there, I became curious. So, being cautious not to step on any blood, I lifted my boot toe on the tip of the blanket that covered the head, just to see if I recognized the face of the inmate. At that moment, many inmates began to shout out at me that I was disrespecting the body. Then I thought, maybe I should've bent down close and used my hand to move the blanket instead of my toe, but then I could risk slipping on that large pool of blood. It was too late; and no, I didn't recognize him. Finally, the Medical Examiner arrived, and the body was removed. All the blood was cleaned away; and once again, it was business as usual. The inmates were locked out. I looked at my watch, and whatta ya know, it was time for lunch.

I got home that evening and my wife complained about her day. I listened, but my instinct prevented me from telling her about mine. Those types of days come with the territory. I knew there would be many more unusual days, or should I say usual days, due to the nature of the job. This decision was made many times during my time in the jail system. I never told her about the bloody beat-ups that sometimes were necessary for compliance with the rules or the assaults on the staff that occurred frequently. I never told her about the young Hispanic inmate who was murdered in his cell with a sharpened 15-inch stainless steel kitchen ladle jammed down his neck, all the way into his chest. His eyes still open, staring blankly, the walls of the cell smeared with his blood. His fate was sealed when he insisted on changing the TV channel a little too often. By the way, Captain Hollywood sent me to that one, too.

People ask me, "How did you do a job like that?" Even retired police officers wondered. All I know is when my mother told me that I had changed, I knew what she meant. It's a little like a soldier coming home from war. You're never the same. It hardens you just a little.

It's ironic that while growing up with my older brother, she used to call me the soft one. Some people have a knack for adjusting to their environment. I happened to be one. Now, I'm out longer than I was in. I think my mom was right. I'm still the soft one.

HOLLYWOOD

The Vernon Bain Detention Center was a repurposed ferry boat that was named after warden Vernon Bain, AKA Hollywood. Hollywood Bain is no longer with us. Everyone knows that you don't get anything named after you while you're still alive unless you've donated millions to some sort of structure or cause.

You might ask, "Why the nickname Hollywood?" Bain came up through the ranks in the NYC Department of Correction very quickly, from captain to the high rank of supervising warden at the young age of 42.

Hollywood was a sight to behold as he strolled through the prison corridors wearing the brim of his eight-point hat practically touching the tip of his nose. You could barely see his beady eyes peering down at you while barking questions and orders with that baritone voice of his as he moved at a slow and steady pace. He possessed a unique talent of projecting total dominance over you and at the same time receiving the respect and adulation that he seemed to crave. The image he displayed was stardom, with his short curly hair always having a sheen to it. With his pencil thin mustache and smooth chocolate skin, he was an actor playing his part, always in character; hence the name Hollywood.

Floating jail named after Hollywood

He used the inmates to his advantage by secretly rewarding some with cigarettes, the jail gold, for information leading to a planned escape or anything that would jeopardize the security of the institution. This technique produced great results.

Tragically, at the peak of his career, Hollywood's life ended with an unfortunate auto accident, still at only 42. A tremendous and shocking loss to everyone throughout the department. We recalled the image of his power and control which he never really used to hurt anyone if he could help it.

There were so many people attending his funeral that it looked like some sort of large demonstration. Throngs of people, shoulder to shoulder. Too many for all to enter the church service. Like a famous actor who died too soon, he was certain to win the lifetime achievement award for best performance deserving an Oscar. His persona will always be remembered.

Hollywood, we learned a lot from you. You showed us how to be a good supervisor. I guess you could say, "YOU TAUGHT US HOW TO ACT."

Sometimes you knowingly walk into danger. That's the nature of things to earn your pay. The potential for injury was a reality every moment within the brick and steel enclosure.

A DAY AT THE OFFICE

Correction officers went to work never knowing what to expect, over and above the usual level of stress, which was a given in a jail atmosphere. One minute, you could be eating your meal, when the alarm would ring. This meant there was violence in one of the areas of the jail. When the alarm sounded, the first person who knew where the trouble was would shout it out; and we would pass the word along until we knew where to respond. Upon arriving on the scene, we never knew what we would encounter. There wasn't time to don any protective equipment. Alarms always meant that some sort of violence was occurring. It was either two inmates fighting each other with their fists or a group battling each other. Occasionally, an officer was being assaulted.

Sometimes there were makeshift weapons involved. We called these weapons shivs. They were usually crafted from pieces of metal taken from bucket handles or from the inner workings of old typewriters. These shivs would be made of just about anything they could get their hands on that could cause harm when sharpened. Sharpening was done by scraping the metal object against the concrete floor or walls until they were razor sharp. Handles for these weapons would be fashioned from torn pieces of bed sheets. Finding these shivs and any other contraband, such as drugs and hypo needles, took some concentration to expose where they were hidden. On a typical search, my job was to check the outlying areas for this contraband while other officers strip-searched inmates and their cells. I would find shivs, pieces of hacksaws, even screwdrivers that were sharpened to spear-like edges. They were hidden in places like the stairwell ledges that led to the tiers. Sometimes, they would be tied and sunk into the shower drains, behind wall light plates, slop sinks, and picture frames. There were hypo needles in small plastic bags stuffed inside talcum powder containers. Some were hidden along the toilet rims, anyplace where they thought you wouldn't think to look.

I became very adept at thinking like the enemy and found most of the contraband, but then the whole process would begin again. They'd just make more, keeping us busy. My philosophy became, "Look for it wherever it would fit," and that was in many nooks and crannies.

If we noticed an inmate who possessed excessive linen in his cell, it was an indication that a possible escape was being planned. Tying together bed sheets was great for scaling down to the ground from a high window or roof.

———————

Inmates were our bread and butter, so keeping them safe and armed with toothpaste and toilet paper was part of our jobs. If a resident happened to commit suicide in your area of supervision, it could be a very bad day for you. It all depended on how the deed was done. OD'ing is something that you may not have prevented; but if he happened to have hanged himself, he'd better be warm. If the Medical Examiner's report determined that the time of death had been more than the hour since you found the body, there would be no defense or alibi, especially when the log book containing the times of your half-hour tours indicated that you walked passed a swinging corpse two or three times without noticing it.

To cope, we try to expect the unexpected. Certain events would test your metal. Officer Tom routinely took his lunch break every day at the same time downstairs on a narrow bench relaxing in front of his locker, eating his ham sandwich, reading the newspaper. On one particular lunch break, he happened to hear a strange sound coming from the next locker room area. At first, he thought that it might be someone using the bathroom commode or maybe one of the guys doing some push ups. The sound was strange enough for him to put down his ham sandwich to investigate further. What he saw next was not only shocking but beyond the realm of reality. A few seconds was all he had time to spring into action. Hanging from his belt by the neck was a fellow officer in uniform committing suicide right before his eyes, gagging with his face a deep purple. Tom quickly proceeded to untie the belt, taking the officer down and screaming for someone to get medical assistance. Tom saved the officer's life, preventing him from ending it all that day. Of course, Tom was rewarded for his swift action that started out as just another lunch break. He received a transfer to the courthouse, along with a better place to eat his lunch, which helped him forget that traumatizing day. Tom lost his taste for ham sandwiches, as well.

The officer who attempted to take his own life had lost his son, killing himself accidentally while playing with his dad's gun. Six months later this officer lost his wife to cancer. You might say probable cause for his actions, not to mention the tattoos of the dates of their deaths on his arm.

As you can see, a correction officer never knows what a day at the office will bring. Hopefully, it brings him back home safely to his very own toothpaste and toilet paper.

WOUNDED KNEE

I t was 1984, the place was the Queens House of Detention. I was
the captain on duty overseeing the fifth and sixth floors. About
8:30 p.m. an alarm sounded from the sixth floor. Two officers and I
responded. We stepped out of the elevator and were confronted by
a six foot three, two-hundred pound inmate who disobeyed the
lock-in procedure. Refusing to walk, he dropped to the floor. At
that point, things became physical. I gave the order to place him
into the elevator. As I assisted, the prisoner grabbed hold of my
crotch with a grip as tight as a locked vice. When I realized where
he had me, I panicked. Everywhere I went, he had to go as well.
While we dragged him, his head was positioned at my left hip.

My first reaction was to punch him several times in his face. His
grip on me remained as tight as ever. Gazing at his face, it seemed
he was looking at nothing, as if I was staring into a shark's eyes.
Now in the elevator, the officers were still beating his body for him
to let me go. Finally, I was free from his grip.

We placed the resident in a holding pen to calm him down and
receive medical attention. His blank stare suggested he was on

psychotropic medication. As anxious as I felt, thinking my genitalia and fatherhood capabilities were over, I later realized that the grip was only on my pants material.

Waking up at home the next morning, I couldn't stand on my right leg. It was swollen, and I was in great pain. I slid down the staircase on my ass. The doctor diagnosed a crushed meniscus and further damage to the right side of the knee from hard blows to the leg. How could I have received these injuries? The inmate didn't hit me. Playing the event back in my mind, the answer came to me. One of the officers had used a weapon called a slapper. A slapper is a non-regulation, leather-bound instrument loaded with lead. Apparently, my body had gotten in the way of the slapper while trying to get the inmate to release his grip.

This now became a compensatory case (on the job injury). Using a slapper was against the rules, but many rules were broken to get the job done. I had to explain my injury in order to be compensated and not have the officer disciplined for trying to protect me. The elevator closed in on my leg as we entered. That was my story. Nine years later I finally received surgery and rehabilitation. Situations like this were always part of the unforeseen battles in a correction officer's environment. It wasn't very funny; but after all, it definitely was a knee slapper.

Custody care and control

Our job as correction officers was to maintain control and to ensure that all inmates received what they were entitled to while incarcerated. These included, nutrition, sanitary supplies, and medical attention. Our responsibilities also included ensuring they remained in our custody until due process occurred. Sometimes it would take extra measures to do so.

IT WAS MEANT 2B

B eing a correction officer on Rikers Island was no picnic. I had over three years in and was still changing shifts every week. It was after the 1975 riots when things got a little less stressful. Inmates got what they wanted. One-man cells and plenty of toilet paper. Special meals if you were Jewish or Muslim. Some would turn Muslim just for the better menu. I guess things weren't that good for some of the tenants. At one point, there was a rash of escapes from our old building built in 1933. All of the escapees were leaving via the roof, crawling through the pipe space, and into the narrow vents. Then they would rappel down five stories to the ground with tied-up bed sheets. That was the easy part. The inmates would then have to make it to the water's edge and swim in the dark to the Bronx. Some had to stop at Brothers Island, which was closer and deserted, because they couldn't swim that well. The East River was not an easy swim. This meant that we officers weren't going home too soon, and we'd have to "Beat the Bushes" in case they were still on the Rock and had not yet attempted the water segment of their journey. In the end, we'd either find them hiding on Brothers Island or floating and bloating a few days later. The swim wasn't easy for a novice.

The department assigned two officers from Headquarters to patrol the pipe space behind the cells to check the back walls for any visible hacksaw cuts. One day it came to me, why should Headquarters have to do this in our jail? So, even though that job was not posted as a new position, I went ahead and applied for it. The personnel captain apparently thought it a good idea to have a steady officer in that role. I got the job and couldn't believe it. No one even challenged it even though I had less than four years on the job. The title of my new job was Internal Security. I had to covertly patrol behind the cells' pipe space without the inmates' knowledge, checking to see what they were up to. It also came with a steady day shift including weekends and holidays off. I was finally on the "A Squad." Now I was out of the housing and not having to supervise inmates.

Sometimes toilet bowls were broken or torn out of the wall in the cells. This left a hole exposing the pipe space behind the cell. I would shimmy on top of the pipes above this space so no one would see my legs walking past. I didn't want them to know that I was back there looking for hacksaw cuts in the wall. I also could hear conversations and even see them when I peered through the dusty air vents on the cells' back wall. I didn't have this job for more than three weeks when I got my first victim. It was Willy T., Block #3, Cell 2B4.

———

One day while performing my routine inspection, I noticed a white line on the lower wall fashioned in a crooked circle about 15 inches in diameter. I touched the white stuff and smelled it. My heart started pounding. It was a peppermint smell. "Eureka!" It was

Colgate toothpaste. Willy T. was using it as you would joint compound on sheetrock. I composed myself and left the pipe space to nonchalantly walk by cell 2B4 and act as cool as I could, preventing any suspicion regarding my find. Deep inside, I was about to explode with excitement. As I walked by, I noticed under the bunk bed's rear wall a painted mural to camouflage his plans. "Bingo," it was confirmed. I couldn't wait to tell my boss, Security Captain Bains. When I did, a massive search of the area was organized. Sure enough, Willy T.'s Cell 2B4 was busted; and I was the guy who finally caught the horse before it left the barn.

On Rikers Island, all personnel had to park their vehicles in a lot and then take a bus to their respective buildings and lockers. While riding on the bus the next morning, everyone was joking and razzing me because of the hole in the wall I had found. Finally, I realized why. *The Daily News* and the *New York Post* had a featured cartoon of a fat correction officer looking at a big hole in a cell wall. I'd like to make it clear. I was only 144 pounds at the time. The *Miami Herald* even sent me a letter trying to sell me a metal detector. My 15 minutes of fame became more than that as the years went by. I busted everyone who attempted to escape with a hacksaw. Only two had made it, and it happened while I was on vacation. My peers had nicknames for me. "Pete the Hammer" was one of them because I carried a rubber hammer to hit any loose cell bars that might've been hacksawed. I was also called "The House Mouse" because I knew every inch of that place.

As a result of this event, I was subpoenaed to testify before the grand jury. Willy T. was found guilty of attempted escape and got more time. Willy T. was found to have a schedule of the tides, cash, a knife, and BVD underpants sewed to a black plastic garbage bag for headgear so that he would blend in with the waves and wouldn't be seen while swimming in the night.

Every time I would find a hacksaw cut behind a cell, I signed the back wall with my initials and dated it with a piece of chalk. I wonder if that signature is still there, PK 2B4. Even if it isn't, it was all meant "To Be."

MISTAKEN IDENTITY

During my career as a correction officer, I had a specialty job assignment that required me to covertly patrol the pipe spaces. These areas were actually the rear walls of inmate cells in the housing areas. These housing areas were numbered and were called blocks.

Each block housed 240 inmates. Blocks 2,3,4,5, 7, and 8 were home to the general population. These were inmates who were awaiting trial for their cases. Block 6 housed inmates who were already sentenced to one year or less. They were the workers who would mop the jail corridors twice a day. Some worked in the kitchen areas or the clothes box which provided clothing and shoes for the indigent. They were all, of course, under the supervision of a correction officer at all times. The Block 6 people were considered low risk and were not expected to cause trouble or be likely to attempt an escape.

The last two housing areas were a little more special than the rest. They were block 1A and 1B. 1A had the more serious offenders with a much higher bail or were in a category called Protective

Custody. Protective Custody inmates were those people who were accused of committing crimes that were looked upon by the general population as being deviant or against a type of street code that was highly frowned upon. A few examples would be raping or murdering a child or an elderly grandmother. There were others, but you get the picture. Arrested law enforcement officers also had their own section in protective custody. If these criminals were placed in the general population, they would be in danger of being killed, seriously injured or, in jail terms, become someone's bitch. Our job was to protect the inmates. Hence, Protective Custody was established.

The last and most interesting was Block 1B. It was made up of one tier on ground level and the closest to the administrative area. It housed the most dangerous and notorious inmates. If an alarm was sounded for a response to 1B, it would be very quick. The 1B residents were considered high priority because all were either former escapees or had attempted an escape that failed. All were facing 25 to life and trying to get some unauthorized fresh air and swimming exercise in the East River. They all had one thing in common and that was not to spend their remaining years away from society.

They were being told when and how much they could eat, when to go to sleep, and when they could have a visitor.

———————

I checked 1B's rear walls every day, and for good reason. I discovered I could enter Block 1B without being seen walking through the only entrance into the area and having them know that I was around. Even if they were planning or working on an escape, they would wait until I was gone, of course. Block 1A, which was next door, happened to have a hatch door in the floor of its pipe space which led directly to 1B's pipe space. It was like being invisible and perfect for my objective.

One day, as I entered 1B through 1A, I saw what looked like some light glimmering through the metal vent behind cell 12. It came from the edge of the metal vent that was behind each cell for ventilation. 1B was the only area that had a one-foot-thick concrete rear wall of all the cells. The vents were the only metal in that wall. I had gotten permission to work late that day to further investigate the extra light coming through the vent. The evening shift, which was 4:00 to 12:00, was the noisiest in the housing areas because all of the TVs and radios were on simultaneously, bringing the noise level to the max. This was the inmate's time to commence sharpening their shivs and hacksaw the bars to prep for war or escape.

I would wait until the chow period was over. Then I, Pete the Sneak, went to my position behind 1B cell 12. This cell belonged to Pablo Sanchez, AKA murderer and former escapee, and the one with the curious light shining through. I heard a raspy sound along with a four-inch piece of hacksaw moving in and out of that space in the vent to the beat of 4/4 time, right past my nose. It sounded like music to my ears. After the sawing was done for the night, I sat on the water pipe and peered through the vent holes. They were stuffed with dust, but I could see and hear well enough. I saw Sanchez take three pieces of hacksaw, a screwdriver, and a sharpened shiv and place them into a wet plastic bag. He tied the ends to secure them.

Noticing that the bag was wet told me he must be hiding the contraband in the toilet or sink, somewhere near water, and most likely outside his cell because we searched cells on a regular basis and would have discovered it eventually. The next morning a surprise search was ordered. One of the guys from the Maintenance

Department took apart the shower drain cover which was outside the cells on the tier to discover the package we were looking for hanging down, tied to the drain below the base of the shower floor. The vent was repaired. My follow up that night was to return to the scene of the crime to make sure that I didn't miss anything. What happened next took me by surprise, but it showed me that I really was "Sneaky Pete."

Again, I sat on the water pipe being very conscious not to cough or make any kind of sound. Inmate Sanchez held a meeting with two of his boys, co-conspirators no doubt.

The subject was about who on the tier gave them up. After a short process of elimination, they came to the conclusion that it was Shorty in cell 4 who was the rat. The next thing I heard was Shorty begging for his life and getting beaten and cut pretty badly. Shorty took a ride to the hospital and survived the attack. When he returned, he went to Protective Custody in Block 1A. Sneaking from 1A to 1B via the hatch door became instrumental in catching these thugs off guard and foiling their escape plans. Inmates can be pretty cagey, but I was cagier. Sometimes you have to think like the enemy in order to beat them at their game. Mistaken identity by Sanchez and his boys at Shorty's expense was the department's gain. Elation for me winning the game of good versus evil and keeping a murderer where he belongs. Think about it, if he didn't commit the crime, then why would he want to escape before his trial to most likely kill again? I think, in this case, his identity had not been mistaken. As far as Shorty and I were concerned, Shorty had been mistaken for a rat, and my identity was never revealed.

Score one for the "Blue Team."

VISITS

At least once a week, the incarcerated were permitted to have friends and family visit in a large room just inside the housing area. Many picnic tables and chairs were set up to accommodate several visitors at once. They were searched via magnetometers and wands, along with their personal belongings. This procedure took place before they boarded the bus that transported them to the housing area where the visits would take place.

On the other side of the walls, the inmates who had visitors were stripped of their clothing and required to wear the institutional green jumpsuit. The rules were simple. You had to be reasonably quiet enough so as not to disturb other visitors. You were to keep seated until the visit ended. Afterwards, inmates were searched again prior to changing back to their clothing.

Occasionally, there were disturbances in the visit room. Attempted assaults on a wife or girlfriend accused of infidelity by an inmate would be one of the reasons. Of course, when this occurred, the visit would be immediately terminated. My one obvious observation was that there were very few, if any, males coming to visit these jailed men. It was almost always women and children. The most logical reason was that the men, or as the women put it, the father of their children, were the incarcerated. Marriage certificates were hardly in the equation. If there were brothers, uncles, or grown sons, etc. they just weren't there. These were mostly low-income minorities taking trains and buses to get to the foot of the Rikers bridge then to be transported to the housing areas by correction buses.

What kind of moms and dads did these prisoners have while growing up? How did they end up in this place, and why? Most did not have a father figure to guide and teach them right from wrong. If they did, perhaps they wouldn't have gone down the path that led them to just a roll of toilet paper and a cheap toothbrush.

I had two parents in my household. My mother, and a father I only saw on Saturdays. This was because he worked the night shift and slept most of the day. In spite of his work schedule, he was a strong presence in my family.

I also wound up in jail, but at least I had the keys.

FATHERHOOD

W hen my son Paul was born I was thirty-one years old and married for four years. Becoming a parent or father is one of life's true turning points. It literally changes your way of thinking forever. This was real responsibility now. His life and wellbeing were totally dependent on my wife Maria and me. Made from us, looked like us, really a little me. Just minutes after entering the world I rubbed his little purple hands and purple feet. Watching them change to pink, talking to him all the while. It seemed as if he was actually listening and turning his head toward my voice. That was an exciting and wonderful time for me. That day I became a different man.

Some nights I would stand in the bedroom rocking him to sleep. This would give the wife a much-needed rest while giving me a feeling of deep satisfaction. I really felt what love was.

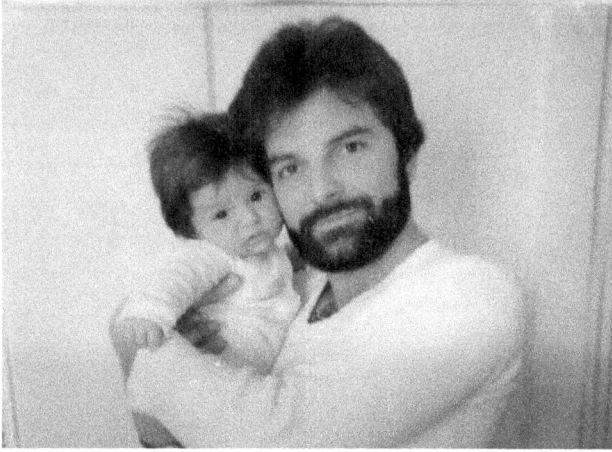

My son at three months, and me.

Nineteen months later, we were blessed with our daughter Stephanie. Perfect, a boy and a girl. They both gave us four beautiful grandchildren; three girls and a boy. Our hopes and dreams were fulfilled. Love was here to stay.

My daughter Stephanie and me, circa 1989.

ME AND DAD

My dad and I never had much of a father and son thing
going.

Let me explain. I had a brother who was a little over three years
older than me. My dad's way of thinking was that you do
everything with your first son, like taking him out with you, letting
him hang around with you and your friends, etc. Dad bought my
brother Alex a baseball bat and a glove at three weeks old. Boy, he
must have been excited about having a son.

Alex told me all sorts of stories about him and dad. Yes, you could
say I was a little starved for dad's affection. I remember when Alex
was hospitalized with appendicitis. Dad took me for an egg cream
soda across the street from the hospital. That felt as good as the egg
cream tasted. Dad worked nights and never really paid any
attention to what baseball team I was on or what position I played.
The funny part was, of the two sons, I was the athletic one. I guess
pop bought the bat and glove for the wrong guy.

As life would have it, in some ways these experiences made me more independent. My brother had a troublesome life that hurt my parents. I, on the other hand, did alright. No divorce, two great, smart healthy kids, and a house. Everything opposite of Alex's experiences. The lesson is that no matter how many children you have, each one has their own attributes that parents should acknowledge. Everyone has good and bad experiences that they'll never forget. They are ingrained into you.

These memories become part of us and affect our behavior in life. Good or bad, they're all life lessons.

What I didn't share about dad is that he didn't have a dad to emulate. I thought about that later in life. It was my way of forgiving him. He was a good-natured guy. I showed him what I missed by taking him to ballgames and buying him a hotdog and a beer. Dad was the godfather of my daughter, and you know what? I think he finally acknowledged and recognized his younger son's attributes. Life is good.

Dad and me at home.

I was forty-one when Dad got sick. He had lung cancer, and it was the worst kind. All the years smoking filter-less cigarettes got to him at the age of seventy-seven. Towards the end the thing that surprised me most was how he accepted his illness and actually welcomed death. I remember him repeatedly saying that he wanted to die. He didn't show any fear; and it seemed he really meant it. His reasoning was that his quality of life was gone for good. There wasn't any point in living without the ability to be free from pain and just doing the everyday things that he did. It only was to get worse. Maybe his strength came from his world war two experience, I don't really know. It opened my eyes about Dad's strength that I never knew. I admired him for his attitude and strength towards death.

I only saw Dad cry once. That was when he and I drove my brother Alex to the Port Authority bus terminal. Alex was leaving to go to war in Vietnam. Dad knew what war was all about; he being a purple heart recipient himself in WWII. He didn't know if he would ever see his first-born son alive again. That must have been a horrific feeling for him. A year or so later Alex returned alive and well.

Dad's WWII army photo.

At Dad's funeral when the bugler was playing taps. I and everyone else were bowing their heads or had their hand on their hearts, including myself, in respect for my decorated soldier father. I peeked up and saw that my brother Alex did not have his hand on his heart. He was saluting Dad as one soldier to another. My heart almost fell out of my chest and it took great effort not to cry when I saw that. That special bond that they had come back to haunt me once again; but at the same time, it was beautiful to see and remember.

Alex has also left this world and is with Dad once again. Two soldiers, more importantly, father and son. There's something comforting in that thought.

OBLIGATION

In life, there are good times and times that are not so good. When it comes to caring for an aging parent, it can be stressful and exhausting, to say the least. It's something that's not only painful, but difficult, especially when it affects the mind of the one aging.

Yes, it is a burden for the caregiver; but what else can you do? You have to stick it out until the end. The end, sorry to say, becomes a relief, although sad at the same time. That may sound harsh; but if you're honest with yourself, it's the reality. I know, I've been to that place. For some, it lasts for a short period of time. In my case, it was four years of pain to my core. The people that suffer the most are the ones who can't afford the thousands of dollars to have others do the dirty work of feeding, bathing and overall TLC that's involved.

It's family, and yes, there is much guilt involved. You think to yourself that you were brought into this world and reared by your parents. Now it's time for the payback, only it's not as comforting and happy.

After all, someday our time will come. When and how, we can't really know. So, we do what we must because that is life, and along with it, death.

PILGRIMAGE

Thirty-four years ago I lived in an apartment on Queens Boulevard. My fiancé, Maria, lived there with me. It was a Friday, and we were getting married that Sunday in a church with a reception. I was on my way home from work; and as I pulled up to the front of my building, I saw police cars. I asked Mr. Hedgcock's son, who owned the florist shop next door, what had happened. He replied, "They robbed Pete's apartment." He knew that my name was Pete, so I assumed it was another Pete who was robbed.

When I got to my apartment, Maria was crying; and there were at least six cops and detectives inside dusting the place for prints. Maria came home to find the apartment door ajar, thinking that I had arrived home early. Instead, she found the place ransacked. The gifts for the best man and maid of honor were gone with only the torn wrappings left on the dresser. Maria's diamond earrings that she was to wear with her wedding dress and the rest of the jewelry were also gone, including our wedding rings. The thieves took my favorite deerskin jacket and a small caliber gun and used my Yves St. Laurant bed sheets to carry it all out in. The one thing they missed deep in my drawer was six hundred dollars in cash. The next day we used that to buy plain gold wedding rings so that we had something to place on our fingers at the altar. IOUs were given to the best man and maid of honor and we got married.

The wedding was to be an outdoor reception in a rose garden, but it poured that day so we had to have it indoors as a last resort.

The robbery occurred in the daytime. The door had not been jimmied or damaged in any way, suggesting keys were used to enter. I didn't mention that my one and only brother happened to be a heroin addict and did a year in prison for armed robbery. He was the real estate agent who arranged for me to rent my apartment and was very familiar with the area. I had asked my mother if she still had the extra apartment keys that I gave her to hold in case I lost them. Mom denied ever having them or said she couldn't find them.

My brother attended the wedding, and Maria and I went on to Hawaii for our honeymoon. I never thought it appropriate to confront or possibly falsely accuse him of being involved that day 34 years ago. He later replaced heroin with alcohol. Alex died several years ago of liver complications just short of his sixtieth birthday. I recently returned to the scene of the crime. The old apartment building now has a buzzer-type security system in order to gain access inside. I remembered that in the back where the garages were, the basement door was always open for people to get in after parking their cars. Sure enough, it still was. I took the elevator up to apartment 2J, right across from the garbage shoot. Then I paid a visit next door to Hedgecock's florist, and Hedgecock's son, the one who told me about Pete's apartment being robbed, was still there, now looking exactly like his father did back then. I tried to jog his memory about what had happened that day long ago. What I really wanted to know was if he really had known something that he didn't disclose about the robbery. He knew my brother from the real estate days. I just wanted to know for sure who did or didn't commit that crime. There was no break-in. Mom didn't have the extra keys. It was too long ago; Hedgecock hardly remembered me.

Before he died, my brother's last words were, "Peter, I can't answer your questions now." What was he thinking? What was I supposed to ask? I didn't ask. Did I really want to know? He died an hour later.

They say your gut is always right. It will forever be a mystery, and I'll have to leave it at that; but damn, I miss my big brother.

ME AND MOM

Ever since I could remember, Mom was the head of the household and captain of the ship. Dad had enough on his plate working the night shift, arriving home at 11:00 a.m. and eating a meal that mom would prepare for him, and then sleeping until dinner. This left mom to handle my brother and me with our everyday needs. I can remember when I was very young watching movies on TV with mom, crying together when the tearjerkers came on. We would wipe our tears together. Mom would always say, "Okay, get the tissues out." Then we would laugh together.

Once, while jumping on my bed, I lost my balance and fell into a cast-iron radiator, hitting my head. I was bleeding and she went into action, cutting my hair and patching me up.

When I grew older and moved out, she always had a care package for me with food, toilet paper, and clean clothes folded in a laundry bag for a small fee of ten dollars a week, only to return it to me with interest, which only a mother would do.

My brother Alex, mom and me

After dad died, I had the honor of watching over mom. My brother lived hours away. As she got older, I'd take her shopping for food or clothing and have her over the house for every family event and holiday. In her eighties, Mom's health declined physically, depending more on medications. She eventually went into the hospital for emergency surgery that left her with a colostomy bag, and she never saw her home again. Within the next six years, mom developed dementia, along with the loss of her balance. She lived in three different nursing homes until her death at age 93. I had been chosen by the gods to be the person to witness her life end so sadly. It was agonizing to watch and to suffer along with her. This had been such an undeserving end for someone who shouldn't have had to slowly die this way. It was so long a process, and it became very difficult to endure. Many times I would look up to God but would never ask for what I was thinking, to be relieved of this burden. That would have been selfish.

Mom died a week before Christmas. As soon as I was notified, I rushed to see her. When I arrived, the curtain was drawn around her and no one was there to greet me. I opened the curtain and kissed her forehead. She was still warm. I thought to myself, is she really gone? I felt that, somehow, maybe she could at least still hear me. I said goodbye and apologized for not letting on that my brother, her oldest son, had passed away four years before her. I told her that she would have done the same for me. Now she could be with him and laugh with him, as she always did. I felt her again, and this time my kiss on her forehead was cold. Maybe she did hear me.

Mom standing by Hellgate Bridge, circa 1940

The lesson in all this? I guess we suffered through it together, and now we both were free. Okay, Mom, it was time to get the tissues out. Except this time would be our last. Mom couldn't cry anymore, and oddly enough, neither could I.

TISSUE PAPER PATTY

When we were 12 or 13 years old, and after the sun went down, we couldn't play stickball until the next day. This left us little choice but to hang out with the girls. We played hopscotch, hide and go seek, or just hung around and watched each other trying to find ourselves as teens.

I found myself attracted to Mary only because she was attracted to me. Girls usually matured mentally and sometimes physically before most boys. Since Mary liked me and had bloomed nicely up top, I went for her. I eventually asked her to go steady and nervously bought her an ankle bracelet to confirm our commitment. Shortly afterwards we broke up since she wouldn't allow me to get to first base. She didn't take it too well and cried her eyes out.

There was another girl in our group of friends, Patty. She wasn't as fortunate as Mary when it came to breast development. Patty became so frustrated and depressed that she took to stuffing her training bra with tissue paper that she didn't conceal too well. Thus, the nickname "Tissue Paper Patty." Poor Patty, it must have been so hard for her. She also had a bad case of psoriasis, to boot. In addition, I don't remember her ever having a personality either.

Fast forward 15 years. As a correction officer on Rikers Island, I had the inmate visitation detail. I watched visitors arriving to see their family and friends who were incarcerated pending trial. I observed one particular visitor who caught my eye. I had to rub my eyes once or twice, realizing who I saw visiting an accused murderer and former escapee housed in 1B. It was none other than Tissue Paper Patty. Looking her over, she was attractively built. Patty and I recognized each other. I said hello, but Patty didn't say much. I guess her personality had not changed except for her very large breasts staring back at me. That was the last time I ever saw Tissue Paper Patty.

As for Mary, I heard that she has issues, like fear of riding in cars and God knows what else. Once, many years ago, her mother told me that Mary should have married me. Knowing what I know now, I'm glad she didn't.

Who knows where or what Patty is doing at this stage of the game. I'm sure she's not visiting her 25 to lifer every week. Then again, who can tell? Maybe she's smuggling hacksaws in cake, instead of tissue paper, for her hubby to escape again. Who knows what's stuffed up there now. All I know is it would take a lot less tissues.

PAYBACK

Most correction officers perform their duties diligently. People who work jobs with a high level of stress have various ways of keeping it together. Unfortunately, when provoked, officers can be just as violent as inmates in a jail environment.

I can remember a time when an inmate attempted to verbally humiliate me in the corridor while waiting to enter his cell block. He was small in stature but had a big mouth. There were several other inmates in line waiting to re-enter their housing area. They watched this little tough guy's performance intently. We called this behavior "grandstanding." I made note of this and easily identified who he was by name and living quarters.

To make sure I had a stress free night's rest, I arranged a plan to retaliate against this resident of our rent-free housing. Later that day with some help from my fellow officers, I had the tough guy escorted to a fictitious interview in the program area while I waited in the rotunda where he had to pass. When he arrived, I confronted him and began to pummel and beat him to the floor. I let it all out, reliving his successful attempt of pushing my buttons. I was seething as I sunk my teeth into his left shoulder. He screamed for someone to get this crazy officer off of him.

When it was over, an infraction was written against him for attempted assault on an officer. A verbal assault counted in my book, but not in the infraction. To me, it was considered an assault on my body because of the internal stress it produced. This can be more serious to a person's health than a black eye or a fat lip.

In the past, I experienced many sleepless nights because of failing to respond to incidents similar to this. I learned that it was not healthy to keep it all inside. I didn't respect myself; it was a terrible feeling.

That night, I slept very well.

FIRST FRIEND

The first friend I ever had was in elementary school. His name was Gary, and he was an only child. He lived in the first house on the block closest to the corner candy store, which also gave him status. As mentioned, Gary had no brothers or sisters. We all know what that gets you—all the toys you ask for and then some. As if that wasn't enough, his grandparents also lived in his house. Talk about spoiled. At the young age of five or six, I discovered the word jealousy.

Gary always had all the toys I wanted—cowboy guns, baseball bat, space helmet, water pistol, and bicycle. You name it, Gary had it. The worst part was that he never gave a crap about them. They would be strewn on his front lawn rusting away in the rain. That was painful for me to see. Since I was the second-born son, and it seemed that my brother got the fun stuff when he was an only child. I guess I was born too late.

Then there was Lila. Ah yes, Lila who happened to be in our class and lived one block away over the deli. Both Gary and I were in love with Lila. She was very pretty and had a cute smile. Her hair, eyes, and lips were perfect. We finally got up the nerve to pass her a love note in class. The next thing you know, we got invited to her birthday party. I was so nervous I hardly said a word to her. Actually, I was so shy I was almost afraid of Lila. As luck would have it, a few years later she moved away, with the chance for some brave guy to ask her out.

Gary was always kind of chubby, and I was as skinny as could be. This automatically gave Gary a pass to abuse me by beating me up whenever he wasn't happy. He had total physical power over me. This abuse went on until we were about 12 years old. I grew a little, and it seemed that Gary shrunk a little.

One day just before a stickball game, he tried to pull his intimidation tactics on me in front of all the guys. Well that was it, the last straw. Seven years of torture came to an end that day. I had been saving it all for this day. I punched his lights out right into Mr. Gaysor's hedges. After that, we went to play stickball with Gary walking behind me. I heard a voice say my name. I turned and it was Gary with his hand extended saying, "Sorry, Pete." Equal at last.

BAD IDEA

In 1974 I was still living with my parents in a modest garden apartment at Astoria, Queens. Rikers Island was less than a two-mile drive to work.

My dad Nick was retired and frequently passed the time spending his allotted allowance from mom at the local OTB. Astoria was known to have a large Greek population, and some called it Little Greece.

Dad was born in Greece and came to the United States at age four. He spoke the Greek language fluently since he was a child. One late afternoon while leaving OTB and walking to his car, a young male approached him speaking in Greek. He called him uncle, demanding my father give up all his money to him. Nick usually would've told the punk to go "eff" himself and keep walking. Since this kid who couldn't speak English was pointing a small-caliber Saturday night special pistol at him, my dad complied and gave up the $320 he had just won.

For some reason, father Nick didn't bother to report this encounter to the police; but inevitably his two sons found out what had happened. His sons being my big brother Alex and me. Of course, this didn't sit too well with Alex and me, so we swore ourselves in as the two famous detectives Sherlock Holmes and Dr. Watson, and got to work.

We knew someone from the neighborhood who also came from Greece named Zeike. He spoke English and was part of the immigrant crowd of Greeks in Astoria. If anyone could help us find out who this dirtbag was, it was Zeike. He was our only shot.

We recruited Zeike, who knew our dad since arriving from Greece years before. It didn't take long for Zeike to produce the first character to us. Alex and I kidnapped him and presented him to our dad for a one-man lineup. Nick looked carefully at him and stated, "No, that's not him." We then let suspect one back into Little Greece. Now the word in the street was out that two guys were looking for the one who robbed the old man at gunpoint.

It took two more days for Zeike to find another guy for us. This time Zeike was sure he found the right one. He pointed to a specific house on 29th Street where this guy was living. Alex and I snatched him and conducted another one-man line up for dad. As soon as our father saw him he shouted, "That's the guy."

It was early afternoon on a nice sunny day. We ordered our father to go back inside the house as we commenced to take care of some business in broad daylight, right in front of our parents' apartment by the curb. Alex snatched my leather-braided, lead-filled blackjack and proceeded to jack the greece ball upside his head and body. I could hardly get a punch in when someone called the police. As we saw the police cruiser pulling up to investigate, we stopped our fury, taking a break. I tinned them (pulled out my shield) and told them everything was cool. They respectfully nodded and left. That's New York for you. We commenced beating the shit out of him. After we got tired, we called pop back outside after watching from the window to come with us to escort the weasel to the 114th Precinct. The detectives recovered some cash and arrested the illegal immigrant. They returned to the Greek's house, recovering the weapon used in the robbery. It was found to be inoperable. These weapons are sometimes called a 'plugged gun." These guns will not fire.

Now that the case was finally closed, I returned to work for my shift the next day. At roll call, the Captain assigned me to the intake block. That was where all incoming inmates freshly arrested got their linen, soap, and toilet paper. They were also assigned a cell.

As I entered the Block, about 10 newbies were waiting for cell assignments to my right. One particular inmate looked very familiar, appearing to be shaking nervously and in shock as he recognized me. However, this time I was wearing a blue uniform with a badge on my chest. Just the look on that Greek's face was good enough for me. I didn't get the chance to give him one more beating so he could remember his "Uncle" Nick and his two sons for the rest of his life. I wouldn't need Zeike to find his ass this time. I'm pretty sure the Greek didn't get much sleep while staying at the inn, fearing the Boogie Man might visit in the middle of the night. He finally was shipped back from whence he came. To Greece forthwith. That's one immigrant who had a bad taste in his mouth about America.

That being his own blood, of course, and just having a "Bad Idea."

MY BIG BRUDDA

W hen I was small and learning to speak, I called my big brother, "brudda." I found out I had a big brudda at the age of two or three. My most vivid memory of him began at about that age. His name was Alex. He was three years and eight months older than me. Alex must've been glad to have a little brother. I was the guy he practiced on to do all his evil deeds. Alex always cheated when playing games with me, especially when playing cards for money. Even when I caught him cheating, I couldn't do anything about it, and he still kept the money.

One time he took my water pistol away from me and emptied it all into my face while he held me down. On one occasion when teasing me, I hit him over his back with a baseball bat. He fell onto the marble coffee table and cracked it in half. It was expensive to repair. Somehow, no one cared that he deserved and asked for it that day except for me. I hit him with a bat, therefore the table damage was my fault.

Around 10 years old, while searching for a lost rubber ball I used to play stickball, I found a cache of fireworks hidden under some rocks. There must've been 10 mats of firecrackers. A mat is a large package holding 100 smaller packs of firecrackers. My first thought was to rush to tell my big brother what I found before someone else got to it. I was sure to impress him with this. He was impressed alright, he took it all. I never saw even one firecracker from my find.

One evening when Alex and I were walking home to have dinner, there were two strange boys about Alex's age walking behind us. One of them had a basketball in his hands and was throwing it against Alex's back. This is when I learned how my brother's thought process worked and how calculating he was. I was scared that both of us were going to get beat up by these thugs. I remember Alex just turning around slightly to get a glimpse of these guys. We made it safely to the house. My brother just happened to be, and always was, one of the toughest sons of a bitch's I knew. For him not to take action was disappointing, even though I was frightened at the time. It turned out that Alex's train of thought was that his little brother was with him and he would take care of business later. That was why he turned to get a good look at those fools. This basketball bouncer was new to the neighborhood and must have been tough where he came from. I guess he was vying to be the new sheriff in town. Two days later both were the new victims in town. Alex got each one of them alone, mano a mano, and wiped the streets with them, leaving Mr. Tough Guy for last just so he could sweat it out knowing it was coming. Boy, was I proud to be his little brother.

One time I went with Alex to watch him play football with his team when I was 15 years old. This game was taking place in a depressed area of Queens. Alex wore gloves and placed many small rocks inside so that he could punch and hopefully injure his opponent at the line of scrimmage. Not too many plays into the game, the Ref blew his whistle after a play; and just like in slow motion, Alex's rock-filled gloves came crashing down on this big 400 pound, six foot five monster. At that moment, war had been declared. The monster took off his helmet, picked up a nearby bicycle, and threw it at Alex. Alex smartly kept his protective helmet on, caught the bike, and threw it back at the monster. At this point, both teams were scrambling. My brother screamed at me to go and get the car. I was 15 and not prepared to drive the getaway car the way it needed to be driven. Luckily, 18-year-old Donna (who also came to watch the game) saw the panic on my face and was recruited to drive. Somehow we got out of there with the monster chasing Alex down the block. I can still see him getting smaller and smaller through dad's '65 Impala rear window as we drove farther away to safety.

As I approached my late teens, big brother was there for me when I needed him. I happened to have a fist fight in the park while defending a girl's honor who I hardly knew. I was chatting with a girl named Debbie who was dating my good friend, John. A guy I didn't know approached us at the park bench. He started to curse and spit on her. I asked him why didn't he just talk it over with her. He turned to me and said, "If you don't like it, get up off of the bench." I thought about that for two seconds, then got up. In thirty-seconds I was sitting on his chest pummeling his face with my fists. Then, out of nowhere, I had been kicked twice in the face by someone's foot. My lips and eyes were swollen for days. It was this guy's big brother and his friend who saw his little brother getting beaten and decided to kick me in my face. The next day it was Alex and John Bruno to the rescue. Big brother against big brother, who proceeded to even the score. Again, proud to be Alex's little brother.

Maybe this was Alex showing his appreciation for using me to hone his skills as kids, or maybe that's what big brothers are for. He was his own man, for sure. He taught me how to think and try to be strong whenever I felt a weakness of emotion. Now I think of what he would say and do in certain situations. What would be his outlook and opinion? This helps me be strong when problems arise. Sure, he was no angel when it came to other aspects of his life; but boy, I'm glad I had a big brudda and am happy it was him.

THE SPECIAL UNIT

I n the mid-'70s the New York City Police Department established a special emergency service unit called S.W.A.T. (Special Weapons and Tactics). After the prison riot in 1975, with six officers held hostage, our department decided to establish its own emergency service.

At 25 years old, and with only three years on the job, I became one of the first 100 members to be recruited. Our unit was called C.E.R.T. (Correction Emergency Response Team). We began training in the field on Rikers and at nearby Randall's Island where the New York City Fire Department trained. Randall's Island had abandoned, burned-out buildings.

We acted out hostage situations in full protective gear. Training included rappelling from three-story structures and several challenging obstacle courses. Also included in our training, we were instructed to present an image of professionalism as we conducted the special searches.

As a C.E.R.T. member, each of us carried our necessary equipment in our car trunks in order to respond to an emergency event immediately. One evening we received orders to respond to the Bronx House of Detention. We were required to search for a gun that may have been smuggled into the facility. This would be a surprise cell search at 2:00 a.m., thus eliminating the possibility of inmates attempting to move the contraband while locked out. In full riot gear wearing flak jackets and helmets, inmates couldn't identify us, even though we were the same officers they would see on the tier daily.

On searches, officers sometimes would joke and appear not to take it too seriously. As a C.E.R.T. officer, we were taught not to speak unless it was to order inmates to comply. We were serious as hell, acting like soldiers. It was very convincing to the inmates. Sometimes you could hear one of them mumble to the other, "Who are these guys?"

All of the searches were filmed by one of us, ensuring that we didn't act in a way that would give an inmate reason to complain.

A few days before we were to commence the 2:00 a.m. search in the Bronx, an officer was assaulted from behind with a chair at Rikers. Officer Jackson was the one attacked and was in the hospital with back and head injuries. As luck would have it, the Rastafarian inmate who did this to Jackson happened to have been transferred to the Bronx house. Although we were trained to be professional, we did not take it lightly when one of our own was assaulted by an inmate, in this case especially, being hit from behind and admitted to a hospital.

During the search, the Rastafarian in question was identified to be in cell 9, third tier. Inmates were ordered to remain silent and stand outside of the cell while their quarters were being shook down. As officers approached the Rasta's cell, the officer filming happened to turn his camera away for a few seconds. Professionalism took a back seat to revenge that morning. When the camera turned back to a disturbance, the Rasta was being forcefully restrained by three C.E.R.T. officers. According to the official report, the inmate refused to comply with being searched and physically attacked the officers. An infraction was written against him for the assault, and he received medical attention at Kings County Hospital's prison ward.

The following day Officer Jackson enjoyed a visit to his hospital bedside by three of the officers who participated in the special search. They brought a magazine and some chocolates, along with something else housed in a small shoebox. As Jackson opened the box, he was startled at first but understood the meaning. It was a unique gift, but not so pretty. Low and behold, he was staring at a swatch of Rastafarian scalp torn from his attacker. The blood was cleaned from it as best as possible, but it was wrapped very nicely in C.E.R.T. blue tissue paper. All training aside, very professionally done.

There are people you meet that become etched in your memory for life.

JERRY CONDOS

J erry was a Greek boy who lived on my block. He was a year older than me. I met him when I was about 16 years old. Jerry's father was always away working, painting ships. When he was home, he was very strict. Jerry's mom couldn't handle him, and Jerry took full advantage of that.

When I got drunk for the first time, it was with Jerry. We attended a party at a friend's basement. It was a kind of a formal dance with girls. Well, Jerry managed to get his hands on a pint of Southern Comfort whisky, which we sipped before the party. It wasn't that bad going down as it had a sweet taste. We were feeling pretty cool, slow dancing with the girls. So far we were having a good time and feeling a little more mature than the other guys, since they weren't drinking yet. Another stage of growing up, another passage to adulthood. That was fine until Jerry had another brilliant idea. After the Southern Comfort was gone, we acquired some beer for a chaser. We left the party, and that turned out to be a good decision. All of the mothers thought of me as the quiet, shy type, and they liked me. I wouldn't have liked them to see what I looked like later that evening puking some kind of brown foul-smelling substance from mixing Southern Comfort with beer. If you're curious, Jerry was right there competing alongside me.

The next passage to coolness came about two years later when Jerry and I went through the pot stage. Jerry bought a lot of pot because he dropped out of school and worked. Never mind rolling joints, he went right for the old corn cob pipe filled to the brim. He used to pay me in pot to drive him to work. I thought it was a good deal, especially if I picked him up later.

We'd smoke his stash, not mine, on the way home. Jerry was generous that way. Since we were both Greek, we decided to go to church stoned out of our minds. Right in the middle of the sermon, we got the giggles. No, it was more like the laughing fits. People were turning their heads, giving us the evil eye. We would walk outside to compose ourselves; then as soon as we got back inside, the fits would start all over again. It looked to us that the priest was going to send us straight to hell if we didn't get out of there quickly, and that is what we did. On the way out, we felt like the priest and everybody else were chasing after us. I guess the paranoia came with the territory.

Jerry Condos had other talents, as well. He used to turn his eyelids inside out and scare the devil out of all the girls. I think it was Jerry who invented the hole in the pocket trick. That's when he would place his erection through the pocket hole and have Mary and Nancy reach inside to get something for him. He was nuts.

A few years later Jerry would go on to become a full-fledged heroin addict. That was after the alcoholic stage, of course. At the age of 21, he left for Iowa to work, got married, and had a child. A few years later he came back to visit. I noticed Jerry had his left wrist heavily bandaged. He proceeded to tell me in his Iowan accent that he had pistol whipped a guy in a bar. That same guy tried to chop his hand off with a machete a few days later, hence the heavily bandaged wrist.

I heard that Jerry passed away in a hospital some years ago. He couldn't have been more than 50. I guess his organs just couldn't take the abuse anymore. I had some good times with Jerry, until he got too deep into things. I was sorry to hear of his fate but not surprised. Sometimes I wonder if things would have been different if his strict dad wasn't away painting ships so often.

Jerry was a free spirit. Maybe now his dad has got him in check and they're painting ships together. Knowing Jerry, he's trying to figure a way to escape from that ship and his father. I wouldn't be surprised!

THORNS IN MY SIDE

There are evil people in all walks of life, just like Mr. Cotto and Miss Gianedes. In the jails, there were captains and assistant deputy wardens whose only mission was to find faults and write us up. When they were on your tour, the game of cat and mouse came into play. They enjoyed ordering you to explain their observations in a written report. Reports were written on a plain sheet of paper. In the upper right-hand corner were the words, Date-To-From-and Subject. The body of the report was written in pen, very simple but not so neat.

The first boss that comes to mind is Captain Cusak. He was thin, blond, and known for his squeaking orthopedic shoes. Cusak always appeared very nervous and angry at the world, acting like he drank a quart of very strong black coffee. He'd always find something to complain about, whether it was a sloppy office station or a dirty floor. He reminded me of the character Barney Fife from the old *Andy Griffith Show*. But Cusak would be the mean version. Captain H would soften up to you if you showed some balls or if the upper echelon took a liking to you.

Then there was the Assistant Deputy Warden Ford. We called him "The Silver Fox." An older, silver-haired black man who didn't say much, Ford liked to sneak up on us. He would enter the block with his own key during the midnight tour. We, meanwhile, were attempting to take our naps on the hard metal picnic tables in the block. If caught, he would write us up. We devised a counterattack by balancing a metal inmate food tray atop the entrance gate into the block. When "The Fox" quietly opened the gate, the tray would smash to the concrete floor and wake up the mice, along with us jumping out of our skins like jack in the boxes. Most of the time, the control room officer on duty did the right thing by warning us that Ford was on the prowl making his rounds. We quickly learned how to outfox, 'The Silver Fox'.

There was another Assistant Deputy Warden, Abbott. A not so tall, plump Afro-American who we liked to call Idi Amin. Idi Amin was a Ugandan dictator who murdered over 300,000 of his own people and also mutilated his wife. He killed people on live TV and kept photos for his own amusement. Abbott wasn't that bad a person, but more than anything else, just resembled Amin physically. Whenever addressing an officer, he'd call him Tiger. "Keep the gates closed, Tiger! Tiger, make sure the house gang gets that area mopped!"

When I arrived at the Queens House of Detention as a newly promoted captain, Abbott was on my case like a magnet to metal. He'd be scolding me like a child, criticizing my reports for not printing my name under my signature or crossing the T's straight enough.

The Deputy Warden of Security was a former captain from my earlier CHDM command. While he was there, some officers were suspected of vandalizing his car because he was not well-liked by the mostly white officers. The reason for this is that he outwardly showed prejudice towards them.

Before being promoted, I was assigned to Rikers and was considered an asset and in good standing at my former command. I couldn't understand why I was being harassed not only by Abbott, but by other ADWs, as well, who happened to all be black. The only exception being one Italian boss. So it didn't seem so much as a racial thing, but I had to find out what was behind this behavior towards me.

In the past, the Queens House of Detention was considered an easy and quiet place to be assigned. It was called the "White House" because there were very few Afro-American officers working there. Pressure was applied to change this situation. More black and Hispanic officers were being sent to the White House, including brass. Now, minority heads were swelling and I, and any other white guys transferred to the Queens House, were automatic suspects to the vandalism that took place on the Rock. Determined to defend my reputation, I wasn't going to be treated in this way as a captain and, moreover, as a man. I decided to confront each ADW, one by one, to have them explain this unnecessary behavior towards me. This tactic worked, and I eventually became the union delegate for the captains in the jail. I was now accepted and respected in a place now called by some, the "Black House." I'm guessing this was some sort of payback, but for me, the place was like the others, just another jailhouse.

IRON JOHN

I ron John was a correction officer who was big, strong, balding, and wore glasses. To reassure himself of his strength, he would ask you to feel his hard, flexed forearm. If John just met you, he had to show you his tattoo that he was very proud of. First, he would ask, "Have you seen my tattoo yet?" Of course, you hadn't. Then he would eagerly loosen his pant belt, pull up his shirt, and reveal his strangely-placed tattoo of a large eyeball staring back at you. Now, you're thinking that there might be a few cards missing from John's deck.

Once John approved of you as a friend and coworker, he felt obligated to protect you, or as we called it in the workplace, "putting you under his wing," like a bird protecting its fledgling. He always called me "Kiddieboo" which, to him, meant little brother.

One clear summer day, John couldn't wait to finish his midnight to 8:00 shift to attend a BBQ in the borough of Staten Island where he lived. Unfortunately, he and his partner Vinnie were ordered to work a second shift to escort an inmate for medical attention to

Kings County Hospital in Brooklyn. Officers were provided an ambulance-type vehicle to drive themselves and the inmate to and from the hospital. Iron John had his own plan that day. A detour was in order. John's priority was a BBQ in Staten Island before having the inmate treated in Brooklyn.

When John and his partner Vinnie arrived at the BBQ, Vinnie mentioned to John that they couldn't leave the inmate alone in the ambulance since he might have a notion to attempt an escape. John thought for a few seconds and then proceeded to secure the inmate by handcuffing him to the fence of the house while the two enjoyed the food and beautiful weather, of course, bribing the prisoner with a hotdog, chicken leg, and a soda. Now it was time to proceed to the original assignment. After being gone from the institution for more hours then it should've taken, the deputy warden ordered John and Vinnie to each explain in a written report why it had taken them so long to return, generating excessive overtime. The deputy noticed that they were sharing with each other what they were writing. He then ordered them to separate rooms to ensure that there would not be any collusion between the two. Minutes later the deputy overheard John and Vinnie shouting across the rooms to each other to find out what the other was writing.

After the reports were finished, Vinnie was asked why he didn't sign his report. He replied that he couldn't sign it because it was a lie, just as the deputy suspected. The boss appreciated the gesture from Vinnie. In the end, the truth had set them free, well, almost the truth. They forgot to mention the BBQ and handcuffing the prisoner to the fence, the only witness to the truth. I guess that hotdog, a piece of chicken, and a soda went a long way that day.

IRON JOHN HOLDS A CLINIC

Midnight to 8:00 tour, the graveyard shift. Tonight officers John and Al are assigned to Housing Block 2. Arriving at the Block, they take the keys from the 4:00-12:00 officers to verify the body count walking all 12 tiers, counting each inmate, hoping they added up to the same total. If not, off they would go again to run up and down the tiers using their flashlights to recount, ensuring that the bodies weren't dummies or hanging by their necks from bedsheets. Finding a dummy made to look like a sleeping body is a sign of an escape. A cold body hanging could mean an officer's job by not making timely rounds. Okay, the numbers jive, and the count is verified. The 4:00-12:00 shift can go home.

Now it was time for John and Al to have a quiet night with everyone locked in their cells to sleep. Iron John commenced to ready himself for the night, going through his usual ritual by removing his uniform and putting on his pajamas to sleep in an empty cell on the second tier. He would wake up at 6:00 a.m and be dressed back in his uniform in time for the breakfast lock out, except tonight would be different.

John had just gotten comfortable when suddenly one resident began shouting, pleading to be sent to the clinic because of leg pain from a previous gunshot wound. John angrily shouted back for him to wait until the morning lockout. The inmate ignored John's suggestion and shouted several more times, "C.O., I need to go to the clinic." The "B" officer knew that Iron John did not like to be disturbed. Al approached the inmate's cell to warn him not to anger John any further or he might wish that all he had was his leg pain. A few minutes passed, and again the calling out for help persisted, which by now began to awaken other residents. John, boiling red with anger at this point, shouted to the inmate, "Shut up, or I'll come out there and hang your ass." However, the challenge to John was relentless. At that moment, C.O. Al thought he heard some tearing of a material that sounded like the ripping of bed sheets. Al decided to investigate and, surprisingly, saw that it was coming from Iron John's suite. Al couldn't believe what he was witnessing. John was braiding the torn linen into a hangman's noose. At that moment, the entrance gate opened. The meal relief officer, Manning, entered to relieve John for chow. When Manning saw what John was up to, the meal relief was suddenly canceled; and it became an aided and abetted event. Manning opened the inmate's cell who assumed that he was finally going to the clinic; but instead, Manning lifted the wounded resident while John placed the noose around his neck. He then tied the other end of the noose atop the heavy iron gate and let him hang for ten seconds or so. The inmate, now in shock, forgot all about his gunshot wound. The noose was removed from his reddened neck. Iron John then lifted the inmate by his shirt and pants and tossed him like a rag doll over the table that led to that damn clinic. If you mess with Iron John, you might just get what you are, "a pain in the neck." The lesson: do not disturb the disturbed.

HADDA GO

The Iron Man had been on his assignment in Block 4 for three hours. Chow reliefs weren't scheduled for at least another hour. The urge to take a crap came upon John a half-hour ago, and he couldn't wait much longer for his meal relief.

There weren't any private facilities in the Block for an officer to do his business. He wasn't about to take a shit in an empty cell in front of the inmates who were all locked out for recreation. John called for a personal relief, but the control room captain had no one available. He was about to shit his pants if he didn't do something quickly.

The Block's supply closet was to the side of the "A" officers station. He went in, locked the door, grabbed a mop bucket, and commenced to drop a load in it. Now relieved but pissed off, he placed the steamy bucket outside of the block into the corridor. Apparently, Iron John's nickname wasn't because of his iron stomach.

Now totally frustrated, he'd had enough of this hellhole for one day.

The Iron Man needed a break. Finally, his meal relief arrived. While in the mess hall, he met his buddy, Vinnie. John had a crazy idea that would get him out of there and home for a few weeks. He asked Vinnie for a favor and returned to the block with him. He told Vinnie that he was going to place his hand in an open draw at the "A" station and that Vinnie should slam the drawer shut on his hand. The great friend that he was, Vinnie turned his head away, shut his eyes, and granted John's request.

John was out of work for two weeks with full compensatory pay. The official report stated an inmate worker accidentally closed the supply closet on his hand.

Twice in one day, the feeling of desperation took over, with a friend having a hand in it all. A helping hand, if you will.

LARRY LORD

The right screw for the right nuts.

The House of Detention for Men had separate housing areas for certain crimes. These areas were called Protective Custody. An example would be rapists, cop killers, and child abusers. These inmates would not survive in the general population. Even criminals had their rules.

The one protective area that intrigued me the most was in the Block #2A section on the flats. Flats meant that it was the bottom tier of the three. It was 20 cells with one officer assigned to oversee the welfare of the MOs. MOs stood for the mental observation inmates. Some officers would earn a steady tour and housing section for mostly seniority reasons.

There was one particular officer that comes to mind when I think back to the mental observation section. His name was Larry Lord.

Talk about the job fitting the man. Larry Lord was very big in stature, and he wobbled back and forth as he walked. He wore big, long, dirty shoes that pointed left and right as he slowly hobbled to his post. Larry always complained about his "bad feets." You could get seasick watching him sway from left to right. He wore his uniform hat tilted to the left side, and his bulging eyes always looked as though they were halfway out of his head. He never appeared to be clean-shaven and always seemed to have the same amount of stubble to his face. The shirt over his large belly always had a food stain somewhere on it. Larry spoke with a fast mumble, that only his brood of MOs understood; and Larry understood them, as well. Sometimes it seemed that the boss just put a uniform on the largest MO to keep them in check.

His manner gave the impression of the most non-violent, laid-back person in the facility. I bet he made a great grandpappy at home. It was as though he didn't have a care in the world. To see him was like looking at a human cartoon character. Truly a sight to behold.

The best thing about Larry was that he had the most peaceful group of inmates in all the housing areas. It was a job made in heaven for Larry. I suppose we have to just, "Thank the Lord."

Keeping inmates in check was our main objective. It turns out, however, inmates weren't the only ones that needed to be kept in line.

HE'S A PISSER

M y reputation as the Internal Security Officer was peaking. This was because I had thwarted several attempted escapes and was considered sort of a sleuth. I was sneakier than the average conspiring inmate. As a result, I was asked by the deputy warden's office to help solve another problem; and this time it had nothing to do with an inmate.

The deputy warden's staff officer, Jim Hughes, approached me one morning to ask a favor. It was reported to the deputy that someone was urinating in the officer's locker room on a daily basis. The problem was that whoever it was wasn't pissing in the bathroom but chose to piss in a locker room's aisle instead. The room reeked of urine. I thought for a moment and asked Jim how I was to accomplish this. No one pisses when someone's watching. So we decided to go to the area in question. Sure enough, it smelled like the subway platform on the IRT at three in the morning.

Jim's information was that the pisser probably did his deed in the early afternoon because the locker room wasn't crowded then. I canvassed the area and thought for a moment. Then the idea came to me. At the time, I was about 144 pounds soaking wet and ran six miles a day. There was an empty locker adjacent to the aisle that I could try and fit in. I found that once inside I could open it by lifting a lever to get out. I tried it with Jim there in case I got locked in. When I squeezed in, I could barely fit. It was a small space; and I was squished in with every part of my body touching the sides, front, and rear of the locker. It was so tight that my knees were up to my waist. The dry run was over, and we were ready to crack the case.

The next day I got in my upright iron coffin early so that I could wait for the pisser to arrive. Finally, someone came in to change into uniform. It was only the kitchen officer, Terry Monohan. Terry was a bodybuilder with a 28-inch waist and looked just like the muscle guys in the magazines. I was thinking how long would I have to wait in here before the pisser arrived? I peeked through the tiny crevice in the locker watching the Hulk taking his sweet time getting dressed. How long can I be crammed into this space without moving?

Finally, Monohan put his pants on so he could leave the room and get to the kitchen where he worked. I wanted to get on with my investigation. Then he decided to comb his hair. What was next? I found out quickly when Terry unzipped and started urinating into the large soap barrel we used for locker garbage. It was hard to believe what I was witnessing. Not Monohan! The clean-cut, muscle-bound envy of inmates and everyone else. Who would have thought that the Hulk, Hercules, Samson was pissing into the locker room garbage every day? Why? The bathroom was in the next room. Now I'm thinking to myself, if I dare sneeze, cough, or fart my ass is as good as dead. I imagined Monohan getting closer and larger, approaching the sound coming from the seemingly empty locker. Thinking that I was some sort of deviant spying on him, he would have started crushing the locker, first from top to bottom, then from side to side with me still in it, then tossing me into the piss barrel. "Oh, humanity." I felt sweaty all over and held my breath. Wait, he was leaving. I waited a few more minutes to make sure he was gone. Finally, I let myself out.

I reported back to Jim and told him the identity of the pisser. He couldn't believe it was Terry, his Emerald Society buddy. Jim asked, "Are you sure?"

I replied, "Yes, and now my life is in danger." Jim assured me not to worry and has kept his word to this day. The mission was accomplished. The pissing stopped after that day and Terry Monohan went on to become a deputy warden. He got very fat and round. At least now, if he found out how he was caught, he wouldn't be able to catch me. The things we do sometimes just to please the boss. Hopefully, Terry is keeping it in his pants and no one asks me for any more favors. Of course, names have been changed to protect myself and Jim, as well.

This story is true. We've come a long way from a young man being stuffed inside a locker to today's tiny hidden cameras. I think, in this case, a simple memo read at the roll call would have sufficed. Something like, "If you're pissing anywhere other than the bathroom, cease and desist." Then again, Terry never attended roll calls so I guess you've got to plan on a case-by-case basis.

Sometimes you think you know someone, then you find out differently. When you think about it, though, "Isn't it a Pisser?"

BEATING THE BUSHES

⚜

I n the early 1970s, there was a rash of escapes from the oldest facility on Rikers Island. Built in 1933, it was named the House of Detention for Men, sometimes called HDM or the Pen, short for penitentiary.

For operating cell doors

The Pen is where an officer would be transferred when he fucked up somewhere else, similar to an inmate going to the Bing after committing an infraction. As for myself and other new officers, we just pulled the short straw coming straight from the academy.

Most of the escapes occurred in the coldest of winter. Escapees probably thought we'd least expect an exit in the bitter cold. We would don our warmest coats, hats, and gloves to search any hiding places, including the East River shoreline where it was the coldest. Making conditions worse, our supervisors didn't provide us with a cup of hot coffee or a piece of baloney on two slabs of jailhouse bread.

We were left out there for hours without relief, peeing in the bushes if we had to. The captain would make his rounds along the shore in his toasty, heated vehicle, keeping his coffee nice and warm. One resilient officer, Tony Jefferson, decided he'd build a fire in an empty 50-gallon barrel that was left near his post. He was a lean, black officer who every year would bring home several gold medals for running races in the annual police Olympics. Tony somehow acquired a few eggs and began to cook himself a meal while keeping warm. At that moment, the captain stopped his vehicle and demanded that he put out the fire. Jefferson, cold and hungry, angrily lashed out at the captain saying, "Where are you going to send me? To the Pen? I'm already here."

The captain left, probably realizing that Jefferson had a point. Soon after, the freezing escapees were discovered, either being found or volunteering to give up, yearning for three warm meals and a hot shower. As for Tony Jefferson, he never put out the fire.

Now it was time to find out how these inmates managed to get outside in their quest for freedom. Our first order of business was to search their perch, which was the cell, making sure the locking devices were in proper working order. We examined the cell bars using a mallet, hitting each with force, checking to see if any were cut and put back in place with wax or toothpaste, making them appear intact. In the past, cell bars and small window bars leading to the outside had been hacksawed. The openings they made would be for their bodies to fit through a nine-by-nine-inch square. To fit through this small opening, the inmate would lose enough weight and grease their bodies with butter that they saved from daily meals. They'd practice inside the cell using the rungs of the bunk ladder which was about the same size opening of the cut cell bars.

Once this was accomplished, they'd wait for the right correction officers to be on duty, those who were less diligent, to make their escape a reality. These officers would be suspended even though the actual hacksawing took place during several tours with different officers assigned.

Inmates escape at night, so the tour after the lock-in takes the weight. Cutting bars and cell walls was usually done on the noisiest shift, which is the 4:00-12:00 p.m. shift. There was always an inmate assigned to look out for any approaching officer. Escapes are well planned, but rarely successful. Some attempt to swim, only to drown.

When practicing our motto of custody, care, and control, we fail at each at one time or another. All three are a constant challenge. It's mind against mind. A psychological chess match that never ends.

In our younger days, our minds and bodies were stronger. Playing sports after work helped us relieve the tensions of the day. It wouldn't matter if you hit a homerun or struck out. Just playing with coworkers who became friends did the job.

The guys on the softball team were not very different from my childhood friends on the neighborhood stickball team.

STICKBALL

I don't know exactly what my age was when I started playing street stickball, but it was probably around nine years old. There were at least ten of us playing every day. All summer long we'd play from morning till nightfall. We always looked forward to a game, especially if you were a good player. If you were decent, it was a good way to get accepted by the guys.

The worst thing was if you were picked last. We picked teams by having one person toss the bat (which could be a broomstick from grandpa's tomato garden) to another person. After catching the bat with one hand, the pair would alternately place a hand over each other until reaching the top without any of the bat showing. Whoever got to the top of the bat would hold it, while the other tried to kick it out of his hands. Whoever kicked it out got the first choice to pick a player from the group, starting with the best.

There was always that one guy who just wasn't athletic. In our case it was Dominick. Dominick was a year older than most of us and couldn't hit or catch very well, but he could kick your ass. He was the guy who expected to be picked last. I always saw the frustration and sadness in his expression. One day it was my turn to have the first pick. That's right! To the bewilderment and surprise of all, especially Dominick, I chose him first. We won the game, and Dominick did well that day. After that, if anyone picked a fight with me you would have to kick Dominick's ass first. From then on, I had a friend and a protector. Even if we would have lost the game, I still won.

PROPERTY VALUE

⬥

During a conversation about the childhood games we used to play, I thought of my favorite—it was stickball. We lived and played on 23rd Street. It was one way and a very narrow street, wide enough for only one car to pass, making it even more difficult to play. There were cars parked at the curbs on both sides of the street. All of the houses were brick and attached with very little front property. We used the sewer tops as home plate and second base and had to contend with the residential forces of evil. On our first base side, field level, was Mr. Cottto, who looked like one of Hitler's henchmen back in the day. Cotto was a short stocky man with tight thin lips, stern eyes, and always wore dark pants and a white tee shirt, sporting a military-style crew cut. When our ball flew into his yard, he'd storm out like he was going to fight us all. He would just scream, take our broomstick bat, and snap it in half for violating his space. Sometimes when we were playing, we'd see him waiting in the shadows, peeking through his living room curtains, waiting to pounce. He looked so mean and tough, just the sight of him always put the fear of God in us. Every time he came home and parked his car, it seemed all of us stopped breathing until he went inside the house. Mr. Cotto would immediately go right to his battle station behind the living room curtains waiting for another stickball bat kill.

On the opposite side of the street in the left field loge was the old Greek lady, Mrs. Gianeides. When the ball landed on her property, it was a race for the ball. We had to try to retrieve the ball fast enough to beat her from getting to it first. Her weapon was a very large pair of shears that sliced through that Spaulding. Mrs. Gianeides actually would hold it up in the air above her head so we all got a good look at the 26 cent rubber ball turning into two little rubber bowls. It seemed like we watched in slow motion as the two ball halves floated in the air and dropped randomly to the ground.

As time passed Mr. Cotto finally moved away, and the old Greek lady got too old and too slow to bother anymore. We didn't have to play the mouse trying to get the cheese before the cat got us anymore. By then, it was almost time to retire the game and move on to cars and girls.

THE SOFTBALL TEAM

W hen I was in my twenties and thirties, I was a member of a softball team we called COBA. COBA stood for Correction Officers Benevolent Association. We played in an outside league that wasn't associated with our job. If it had been, I doubt that we would be collecting our pensions right now for reasons I will explain in part but not in too much detail. This is only to protect the "not so innocent" which, sorry to say, happened to be the whole damn team. The team only had one strict rule. This rule was that no one was to have any beer, or for that matter anything that would put you in a state of euphoria, hyperactivity, or depression until the game had ended. It was a tough rule, but we all abided by it. We wanted to play at our best and won a few championships in our day. Whether we'd win or lose, all of us looked forward to the after-party that was held right on the field after the game. By then, the beer was ice cold and went down quickly.

After a while, the boys were ready to tease the guys who didn't do so well that day and praise the ones who did. The interesting part of all was that our shenanigans, the good, the bad, and the funny were documented on video, both on and off the field. Rob, who had not been a coworker but our third baseman's cousin, was the director, producer, and commentator of the games and post games. These events were very entertaining for all of us. I think this is because of the nature of our business. It had become a great stress reliever. Imagine, grown men using and believing that a beer bottle was a microphone. When someone had something to say, they would snatch the beer bottle from someone's hand to speak into it as if it were a real microphone. Can you imagine what state of mind you had to be in? Perhaps the best part is that there are nine hours of film that have been preserved from thirty years ago. The fact that we can see how we looked and acted back then is very funny and priceless.

Maybe we could get the team together for just one more game. Have Rob film it and make a documentary of then and now, but who would we play? I think I better get on this one before my knee gives out again. Of course, if and when we do play, the same rule will apply to keep our old winning ways: "Not until after the game." At this point, we might bend the rule a little. It'll be just like old times. But this time, just like the beer, the liniment and ice packs will be cold.

NEW YORK MARATHON

It was 1978, six years on the job. Long-distance running was becoming popular. Marathons were also a growing fad. I began to read many books on the subject. I even read a book titled *Running for Women* to see what the difference was. The only change was one piece of equipment—a sports bra. The purpose was to keep the breasts from the discomfort of too much movement. I wouldn't be needing that yet, at 28. I began jogging on a track wearing baseball cleats, eventually graduating to running shoes. I advanced quickly from two miles to five, then to six. I found this sport helpful to relieve tension. Running kept my mind peaceful and far from the house of pain called jail. Every day, right after work, I'd be on the track working on my distance and speed. My body and mind became addicted. I decided to participate in the annual police Olympics, running the three-miler. This was my first race since the fifty-yard dash in high school. Trying too hard and fast, I experienced muscle spasms so severe that they left me with bruises. I had no choice but to drop out of the race. I was embarrassed and felt that I disappointed my teammates. Finishing the race, to save face, would've been enough.

My co-worker John, also a runner, and his friend John, signed up for the upcoming New York Marathon. Unfortunately, John sustained an injury and was unable to run the race. I volunteered to take his place. The training became more intense. We were running nine miles in Flushing Meadow Park, Queens, where the 1964 World's Fair was held. Then on weekends, it became 13 miles in Brooklyn's Prospect Park. Our preparation was not where it should have been for a 26-mile, 320-yard run.

Race day finally came. It was clear, sunny, and 74 degrees. We drank our black coffee and took the B15 pills that we scored from a friend working in the jail clinic. B15s were supposed to add oxygen to our blood to enhance our performance.

The starting gun was triggered and 18,000 runners began the journey through the five boroughs, beginning at the Verrazano Bridge, winding through Little Italy, and ending in Manhattan. John's starting pace was a bit too fast. I suggested that we slow down. The goal was to finish, not win. Around mile 12, we stopped to pee somewhere against a building and continued on.

About four hours later, I experienced "hitting the wall." It was the infamous point of the race that makes or breaks you. My thighs were in pain and began to feel as if little aliens were attempting to escape my body. Only six miles to go. I didn't want to fail as I did in the police Olympic three-miler. I had to think of something to get through this.

Angry and determined, I began punching the aliens, fighting pain with pain. Getting this far into the race, I had to finish. By running faster, I noticed the pain became tolerable.

John was nowhere in sight, but the finish line was. I passed through the finish line and the clock read four hours and forty minutes. I did it! A stranger covered me with a foil blanket to keep me warm; and I received my medal, verifying my accomplishment. Lost in the crowd there was no one to photograph me after completing such a feat. My wife could not find me with so many people wandering about. The subway was free for marathoners, so I took the train home to recuperate.

The next day, John and I called in sick, still mending from our self-inflicted pain.

The following morning at roll call, the boss announced our accomplishment. Not without a joke, however. He reminded all present that we did not report to work the day before. Two days later, I was back to six miles. After running a marathon, six miles became easy and so did jail. The pain was gone and so was the tension. Jail was easier, too.

LIFE IN THE HOOSEGOW

A fter working as a correction officer and a captain in a jail setting, it was a great relief to finally retire after 20-plus years. The officers and inmates had some things in common while incarcerated together. For one, because of the general atmosphere of confinement, both couldn't wait to get out, even though it was only eight and a half hours for us. There was stress for both. The inmate was stressed for being completely controlled as to when to eat, sleep, exercise, and to be locked in their cells involuntarily. They also had to contemplate and wonder what sentence awaited them for their alleged crime.

As officers, our lives were somewhat controlled, temporarily being confined. There was something called "The Stick List." The stick list was a list of names that were scheduled to have off the following day and were eligible to be "stuck" to work a double shift. The nature of the job required that there always be a certain number of officers available to respond to an alarm. As a result, if someone called in sick or needed a personal emergency day and you were off the next day, you were "it." It became our mini sentence. If you worked the 5:00 a.m. to 1:00 p.m. shift, you were being relieved for your lunch break at 9:30 in the morning. You ate whatever was on the day's menu whether you liked it or not. Sometimes it was something called chipped beef on toast, or what we called "shit on a shingle." Other times, it might be liver that had a curious green tint to it.

Ever since I was a young boy I always hated liver. It's amazing how your taste buds adjust when you're hungry. Inmates that were sentenced to under a year for their crime would prepare and cook the food under the supervision of a civilian cook and a correction officer. Some of these inmates had the detail of mopping the long corridors at least three times a day. At the end of a shift when I got home, my uniform would always stink of the strong odor of the pine soap they used to mop.

To this day, former cops and others ask me how I managed to work in that environment? I guess I was young and a pension at the age of 42 kept me hanging in there. It wasn't easy managing the stress caused by witnessing the most bizarre moments that we had to endure, some that I'd like to forget.

In retrospect, we were adult babysitters for adults who needed direction and structure, having no real training or structure ourselves. We learned as we went along from the older and more experienced officers. It was a world within a world.

We were the government, the judges, the caregivers, and the disciplinarians. The outside world had no idea what went on within those walls, nor did they want to know. Of that, I am certain.

LOOKING BACK ON IT ALL

ooking back on it all, none of us were properly trained for
what we would encounter daily in that jail setting. We were
working in the most troubled detention facility in the system.
Whether we were eating in the mess hall or working in a non-
housing area, we had to jump up and respond when that alarm
went off. All of us went running down the corridor together
towards the housing blocks, relying on someone to shout out where
to respond. Without any riot gear, such as helmets, chest protectors,
and batons, we would burst into the area not knowing what we
would encounter. Mostly, it was inmates fighting each other; and
occasionally an officer would be assaulted. Entering the area, we
would start barking orders to the inmates to hit the ground on their
bellies and place hands behind their heads, whether they were
bleeding or not. A captain would order a lock-in, the injured would
receive medical attention, and a cell search would ensue, including
the external areas for any makeshift weapons. To have this type of
response without body protection was very dangerous and careless.
The mindset was that our response to the unknown situation had to
be swift, for fear of one of our officers being in danger. We always

knew it could be any one of us in harm's way when the alarm went off.

Things have changed since then. Now before anyone goes near a potentially dangerous situation, you must muster and don riot gear, then follow the supervisor's instructions. A captain with at least four to six officers would approach and assess the area to determine whether there was a need for a backup squad. This initial team was called the "Probe Team."

A full-scale riot would call for an escalated plan which would include tear gas and all the officers you could muster. There were important decisions made by more important men. These men were wardens, supervising wardens, all the way up to the Governor.

We were damn lucky to come out unscathed. Glad to be here, looking back on it all.

"The Art of being wise is the art of knowing what to overlook."

William James

I learned early on to keep certain information from friends and loved ones. Over time, this spared them much grief. Being exposed to challenging and unpleasant experiences will humble you.

ROLL CALL / PSYCH I

M y first day as a rookie during roll call, the captain mispronounced my last name. As nervous as I was, I became unsure in responding; but after a slight hesitation, I did. Thirteen years later I found myself in the captain's position conducting roll call every morning at 7:00 a.m. Some officers found it too difficult to pronounce my last name, so instead of Koutsoukos, they addressed me as Captain K. I didn't mind and thought it was kind of cool. What I learned from my own experience is that I would make sure to pronounce each officer's last name correctly. At five minutes before roll call, I'd review any unfamiliar names that I might mispronounce, then take the officer aside and ask how to properly say his name. This practice would bring great satisfaction, and I'm sure it made the officer feel very comfortable, too. I had been in his or her position myself. This simple gesture contributed considerably to the respect I would gain.

As a first-line supervisor, I learned when to be a disciplinarian while remembering that my subordinates were human beings dealing with the stresses of their day. I would remind them not to take kindness for weakness when they attempted to take advantage of me in any way. Not surprisingly, the inmates would use these same tactics all the time.

When an inmate would see a new officer for the first time, he would look him or her over, trying to read their eyes and body language for obvious weaknesses. This was an attempt to take advantage of them any way they could. They would try smuggling contraband, whether it was a sandwich, hacksaw, or even drugs. These tactics were called "getting over on you."

At times N.Y.P.D. officers would deliver an arrested person directly to the intake area at the jail. The intake was where all the arrested would be processed and housed. It included a strip search. They were ordered to stick out their tongue and lift the genitals, turn around, and spread the buttocks apart. All this for the possibility of hidden contraband. The new residents were then given linen, a blanket, a prisoner I.D. and were then sent to an assigned housing area.

On occasion, police officers would be present during a prisoner transfer, witnessing an unpleasant physical altercation between officers and an uncooperative inmate. Many retired police officers have asked me how I could have performed a job like that for 20 years? My reply was that it was not easy. Their role was to arrest the perpetrator, but we had to live with them.

Some people have imagined the tall, burly, tough jailer sporting his baton, beating his prisoner into submission. Admittedly, on rare occasions that became necessary. This job was more of a psychological game than anything else. As an officer, appearing in good physical condition would be enough to prevent being challenged, even if you couldn't fight a lick.

I remember one inmate challenging another, warning him that he could fight. The other retorted, "But can you fight and win?" I thought that response was profound, and when I think of it I knowingly smile.

The job has taught me much about human nature and its frailties. Experiencing the lessons was hell at the time. However, having that knowledge now is priceless.

THE LESSON

On the day tour at the Queens House of Detention, we would conduct a daily search. Most of them would be in the housing areas. The security captain supervised each search. With the absence of the captain who usually had the task, I was asked to conduct the search,

Because of my background from Rikers and expertise in finding hidden weapons, I decided to test the officers participating in the search. The area chosen that day was the law library. When mustering the officers, I explained to them that we had received a tip of a gun or knife secreted somewhere in this area. What I failed to tell them was that prior to the search, I hid three hacksaw blades, a knife, and two sharpened shivs in the library. We proceeded to the eighth floor to commence the search for this dangerous contraband. Most of these officers were the same people that routinely searched every morning, Monday through Friday. They would look behind wall hangings, move furniture, lift typewriters (yes, I said typewriters), and appear to be doing their jobs. After twenty minutes, time was up. Curiously, not one piece of contraband was discovered by the nine officers assigned to the search.

I gave the order for everyone to gather together. Now the lesson began. The first order of business was reminding them that by routinely performing this daily task, they tend to become complacent, minimizing the importance and reasons for these searches. I continued by moving place to place, revealing every piece of contraband they hadn't found which, unfortunately, was all of them. I first threw three hacksaw blades from two different hiding areas to the center of the floor, explaining that this could be your job when the inmates escape on your watch. Continuing, I slammed the two shivs and a knife to the floor. I reminded them that this could be your life or your fellow officer's life.

Lastly, I said to all that they must never forget the importance of their job as correction officers, and I hoped they had learned an important lesson. This time it was the easy way. I prayed that they would never learn this lesson the hard way.

ACTING CLASSES

I t only took the first few years on the job to become a formidable actor. My persona at the workplace became very different as I reached the end of the Rikers Island Bridge, parked my car, and entered the house of pain.

Just like rock bands and actors reaching the stage to perform, I became someone else. In the locker room, I changed from street clothes into my costume. It consisted of a badge, a two-way radio, and a three-inch Boy Scout knife I was to use to cut down an inmate who decided to hang himself. The knife had to be as sharp as my mind while walking among the living dead.

For the next eight hours or more, I must be perceived as confident and self-assured to avoid being taken advantage of. This was part of the underlying stress experienced on the job. I was unaware of the effect it had on my mind and body.

The first time I realized the impact the job had on me was when I went on a three-week vacation to Cape Cod. It took the first two weeks to wind down and relax enough to enjoy it a little. The third and final week, my thoughts were solely on having to return to that place again. It was then that it became very clear why others quit to seek another vocation, unable to stick it out. I had no idea how I was able to survive and continue.

The stress was all-consuming. On the first vacation day, I felt compelled to write a letter to the Correction Commissioner outlining how little the administration thought about the wellbeing of the staff, especially the mental and physical plight of the correction officers.

The inmates received state of the art gym equipment with steel weight plates that enabled some of them to bench press 400 pounds. We got the inmate hand me downs that were rusty and covered with chipped paint. We were forbidden to use them on our 45-minute meal break to relieve our stress. Inmates were deemed more important.

My letter was published in the correction newsletter. It was edited, of course, omitting any blame attributed to the Commissioner. As a result, it did little to change things concerning the potential psychological and physical issues that would arise working in an unpredictable and volatile environment.

My acting roles were varied and changed daily. At times a disciplinarian, ordering inmates to lock into their respective cocoons to verify the body count. Another may be a maintenance man, transferring an inmate to another cell due to a plumbing malfunction.

Then there was the role of a soldier, donned in riot gear, threatening violence if compliance with the rules was not met. To leave all of this at the end of the day was like blowing out a candle, finally releasing the heat.

I have an old friend who is a retired warden. He decided to audition for a part in a local church play. While interviewed, he was asked if he ever acted before. His reply was swift and confident. With a half-smile and sly gaze, he said, "I've been acting for the past 25 years." Yet another role to play. He got the job!

THE HARDWARE

❧

Any job that a person may have requires some kind of equipment or tool to perform their respective vocation. Correction officers have a few specific tools that are staples of the trade. Of course, handcuffs are required for transporting inmates to and from the jails. Leg shackles are used for connecting handcuffs to the ankles to restrict leg movement, limiting one's running ability.

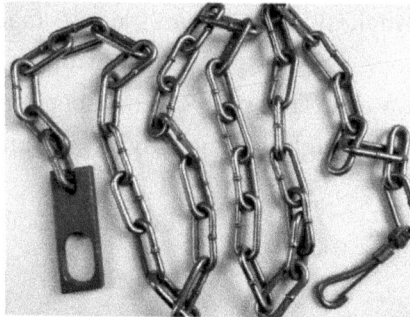

Shackles applied ankles and handcuffs, to prevent running

Many locks and gates inside a prison are controlled by large, thick, solid brass keys called Folger Adams, made in Illinois. These keys are specifically designed to be hard to cut through, difficult to copy, and nearly impossible to hide on an inmate's body.

Folger Adams standard jail keys

Before the 1980s, another tool officers carried was a standard Boy Scout knife with a three-inch blade. This was supposed to be used to cut through a makeshift hangman's noose made from braided bedsheets. The hope was to prevent confronting a cold, purple body swinging in a cell. This type of knife performed very poorly, often failing to saw through the thick, tightly-wound linen.

Boy Scout knife used to cut down hanging inmates.

To improve the capability in cutting down a suicidal hanging attempt, the department invested in a tool that the fire and police departments already had in use. It was used for cutting through accident victims seat belts who were trapped inside their vehicles. It was super sharp and quick. The knife's blade is shaped almost at 360-degree angle, wrapping around its target with great leverage. Its name was the 911 knife, long before the tragic event in 2001 happened. How it got the name is still a mystery.

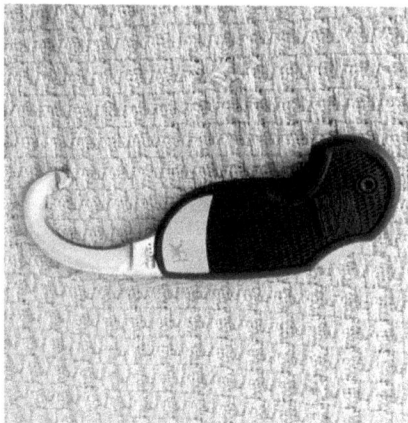

911 knife improvement of boy scout knife, for hang ups

These were just some of the tools we needed and used to help us perform the necessary duties in keeping the boys and girls safe and in line.

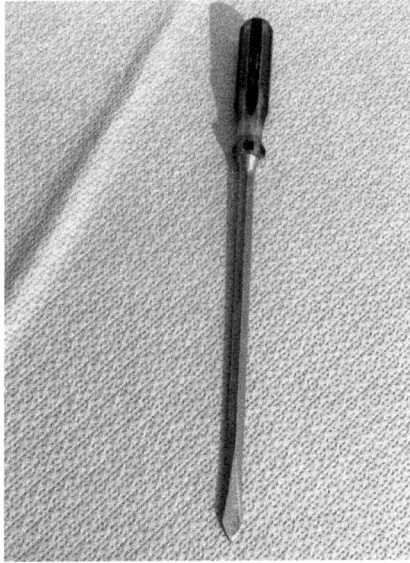

Screwdriver left by maintenance

The most valuable tools we possessed were attitude and body language. It was how we carried ourselves in order to create an image that demanded respect. This also encouraged mindfulness not to push the wrong buttons. We needed to project an aura of superiority. The goal was to treat inmates as though we cared. This behavior went a long way in keeping the peace, even if we might have been acting a bit.

Old corrections patch called 'meatball'

The ultimate tool in the box was our intellect. At times we were craftsmen, even though that tool name was already taken. On the job, this tool was used the most. All the other tools were kept in the box as backup. This approach worked most of the time, but all tools wear out in time.

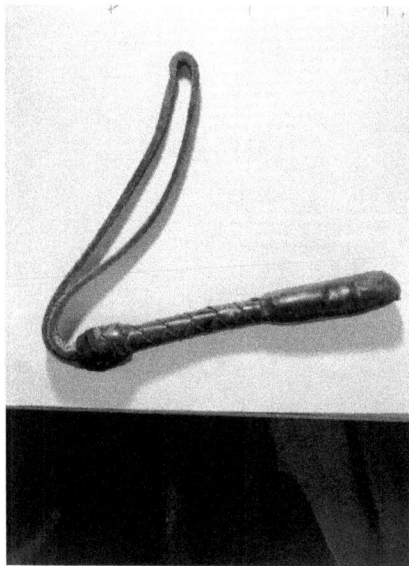

Unauthorized weapon, tightly braided leather covered lead black jack

After 20 years, it was time to leave the shackles, keys, cuffs, and the rest of all the metal that surrounded me. Now it was time to care for my body, mind, and spirit.

HANGING IN THERE

❦

(IN RETROSPECT)

My personality changed from playing stickball in my youth. I was compassionate by nature at an early age by choosing the worst player first in a choose-up game. After experiencing the events I witnessed on the job, I didn't notice the subtle changes in me.

Working 20 plus years as a correction officer is a lot different than doing eight or so. Some bowed out because of the nature of the job, and many were unable to cope for various reasons. Maybe it was the changing of shifts or the physical and mental stress when the alarm sounded. The occasional inmate/officer confrontations could also be a factor. Most likely, it was all of the above.

As for me, I was more resilient at 22, along with many others who stayed to get paid. In return, we paid a price for sticking it out. Not all of us were able to find a cushy job in the maintenance shop, motor pool, transportation, or in headquarters where all entering the island would get screened. You had to have a hook, somebody with influence, to work in any of those places.

Many had a minimum high school education, and some with advanced college or military backgrounds would earn the higher-ranking positions. Some were just better test takers and not necessarily better supervisors. Experiencing the different supervisory styles was an education in itself, by taking the good and bad to formulate your own style. You had to remember that you were once a subordinate, and how you perceived your supervisor's actions and decisions affected the event at hand. That's the way I learned to be a fair supervisor, but I knew how to draw the line when a subordinate thought you were more their friend than their boss. Boss came first, and they had to respect that. If they didn't, they would pay in the end with disciplinary actions against them. That would spell respect or fear, friends came last as a superior.

I survived half my career by looking for escape attempts. Getting that job with a little luck and without having any hooks. The last half of my career, I was a captain supervising officers. After retiring at the age of 42, it took some adjusting to live among the free again and to buy back my former self. I'll be owing that debt until I die. Time heals, but it leaves scars.

Obviously, this job would not be for anyone who couldn't handle the occasional murder or suicide, especially witnessing them in 3D, up close, and for real. This is completely understandable. Not all of us can adjust in our private lives and be able to separate the two.

I suppose I'm one of the lucky ones. I'm now 69, considering the average life expectancy for retired officers is 59. I believe it depends on who you are and how you handled life, death, and the frequent violence that inevitably occurs.

On the job, we did what we had to do to survive. The final reconciliation rests in God's hands.

GLOSSARY OF TERMS

Bang-in artist: Person who calls out sick often, especially on holidays when scheduled to work.

Beating the bushes: Searching the perimeter for escapees.

Blood clot: Considered a curse. Not from a mother's womb. Came from a blood clot. (Rastafarian term)

Bing: Confinement after committing an infraction.

Bug out: A person who is a little off mentally.

Celly: Person who shares a cell. (cellmate).

Chump change: No money to speak of. Very little value.

Collars tight: Deprivation of sexual pleasure.

Crack the crib: Open my cell.

Cramping my style: Getting in the way of someone's agenda.

Crib: Another name for cell quarters.

Crimey: Person who committed the crime with you.

Flats: The lower tier. Ground level.

Getting over: Getting away with something. Having an advantage.

Grandstanding: Bragging or showing off verbally. Wanting to be noticed.

Homey/home slice: A person from the neighborhood.

Hooch: Homemade alcoholic beverage made in jail.

Hook: Someone that can help a person to advance in some way, avoiding proper protocol.

House gang: Three to five trusted inmates that aid the "A" officer for clerical and cleaning of the housing area.

It's your world squirrel/wish I had it like you: Person is on top of the world.

Jodi: A person who has an affair with someone's wife or girlfriend.

Kiddy boo: Nickname meaning pal or little brother.

Locking in or out: Opening and closing of cells for entering or egress.

MOs: Short for Mental Observation inmates.

Mule: One who illegally introduces contraband into a jail facility to an inmate.

On the burn: Punished, out of favor.

Parfait time: Strip search which included an anal search. Called parfait comparing it to the parfait cookie with a jelly center.

Pulling your coat: When someone is giving you a warning about someone or something before it happens.

Selling a ticket: Verbally threatening or challenging someone.

Shirker: A person who avoids work.

Skid: A person who has nothing and has poor sanitary habits.

Skid bid: A sentence that is a year or less.

Stroking or rounding on you: When someone is lying and not telling the truth.

Sucking your teeth: When you are angry or upset.

Tasting: Drinking alcohol.

Tinning someone: Displaying your badge to someone. (Badge is called a Tin.)

ACKNOWLEDGMENTS

This book would never have been published if it weren't for my friend and mentor, Rick Monsour. Rick gave me the courage to make it happen. It's remarkable how much of himself he put into this project.

At times, whenever he appeared, I had the feeling that no one else could see him but me. It was as though he was a spirit or some angelic figure sent to me from somewhere to guide me along this journey. Once I jokingly asked someone in our presence, if they could see him too.

I think it's very rare to meet a person, late in life, that you can add to the short list of true, genuine friends. It's been said, that in your life you can count the number of true friends on one hand. He has taken one, of only three fingers that make up my list. I probably will never fill the remaining two, but who can tell?

We took to each other like bread goes with butter. Rick always appears to be on an even keel. His emotions never go too far over the edge in any direction. In a way, we bonded as if we were each other's therapist.

I didn't mention that Rick happens to be a writing coach, and I a writer, so he tells me. We met by chance, just being at the right place and time. This book became a reality, just like our friendship.

I don't know whom to thank or what to thank, for sending a guy like Rick into my life. He's as authentic as it comes, and I appreciate what he's given me. The gift of confidence in myself as a writer.

Rick, I thank you for being my teacher, mentor and a life-long friend. You helped me learn to like myself more than ever before.

ABOUT THE AUTHOR

Peter grew up in the 1950's and 60's in Astoria Queens N.Y. about a mile from the foot of the Rikers Island bridge. He worked as a Correction Officer from the age of twenty-two and retired at forty-two. Peter lives on Long Island with his wife Maria in their empty nest.

www.ingramcontent.com/pod-product-compliance
Lightning Source LLC
Chambersburg PA
CBHW071858090426

42811CB00004B/660